HOW TO HAVE YOUR CAKE & NOT EAT IT ALL TOO

A Guide To Adult Bulimia Recovery

LaurieAnn Campbell

Visit www.howtohaveyourcake.com

HOW TO HAVE YOUR CAKE AND NOT EAT IT ALL TOO: A Guide To Adult Bulimia
Recovery
www.bullimiaddict.com
Copyright © 2020 LaurieAnn Campbell

ISBN: 9-781777-608415-90000

Limits of Liability and Disclaimer of Warranty

The author and publisher shall not be liable for misuse of the enclosed material.

Warning – Disclaimer

The purpose of this book is to educate and entertain. The author and/or publisher do not guarantee that anyone following these techniques, suggestions, tips, ideas, or strategies will be successful. The author and/or publisher shall have neither liability nor responsibility to anyone with respect to any loss or damage caused, or alleged to be caused, directly or indirectly by the information contained in this book. The author does not claim to be a professional health practitioner. The information in this book is based solely on research.

Publisher Branding You Specialist
Milton, Ontario Canada

Printed in Canada

Table of Contents

ACKNOWLEDGEMENTS

To Suzanne Tarbutt – I am not sure where you are, but you made a very big difference in my life. I wish we had had more time together. You made me realize that the most important thing to stay healthy in more ways than just regarding eating disorders, is to keep people around you who treat you as an equal, who believe in you as you are, to not change for anyone and to make sure to always seek positive people and surroundings.

To Sumit Singh – Thank you for your belief in me, and your interest in finding out more about my bulimia. I met you after my recovery, and you are one of those positive people that I treasure having around me. You have helped keep me motivated in achieving my goals. I love you, my surrogate son. And thank you for the beautiful **book cover**.

To Roy Miller – You have been and are a dear friend. I am so glad we met. You were the first person to interview me on video about my bulimia and my recovery on our Podcast. I appreciate your time and your understanding and acceptance of me for who I am.

To my parents, Ross and Pauline Campbell – I apologize for the worry I put you through. At the time you were dealing with this there was very little information for you to go on to be able to know how to deal with this. I love you and thank you for everything you have done for me in my life.

To my sisters, Janet, Donella, and Laura - Janet, you were wonderful in always accepting me, even when you knew I was struggling. You didn't judge me. You spoke to me about your concerns for my health, and that kindness helped me get through. Donella, always my baby sister, I know it was difficult for you to accept my "disorder", but you never left my side. To Laura, my new and beautiful sister, thank you for listening to me. We met after I recovered, yet you showed interest in the journey I went through to finally recover.

To Doc Grayson – I just have to thank you for being in my life. Again, I was recovered when we met. However, you are the type of person that Suzanne spoke about having in my life. No judgment, positive, and the kindest person I have ever met. You are very dear to me.

To my daughter – Thank you for believing in me. I appreciated your interest and your desire to share my story with your classmates. You knew I was struggling, and you remained strong and supportive. You were the first one to interview me about this. I appreciate you. I see you.

To all my friends along the way – Those who knew, and still remained quiet and supportive, I thank you. You were there as I went through the 30 years, and remained my friends. I so appreciate it. Some of you did not know, or so I would like to believe, yet even if you did, you never harped on me about it, knowing it was my fight to fight. Thank you.

To Hampy – My cartoon character. I know this acknowledgment may sound strange, but having Hampy as a creative outlet throughout my bulimia was very helpful. He was there throughout my journey, from start (in fact I created him the first year of my bulimia) to the end. And still remains.

Life is a journey, and sometimes on that journey we take a turn we would never have anticipated. That turn seems to be innocent at first, then it festers into something perceived to be uncontrollable. When we realize that WE ARE in control of how we behave, what we do, how we do it, we can move back on the right path, turn forward onto a new one, surrounded with belief, positivity, and love.

GENERAL INFORMATION

As many of us know, back in the Roman era, festivities included bountiful food to feast on. Participants were known to binge until full then purge to make room for more. Back then, the behavior was predominantly in men. It was also seen as socially acceptable.

Today, the act of bingeing and purging has taken on a different perspective. It is no longer a festive issue, nor predominant in men. It is estimated that 90% of all cases of bulimia are found in women. It is also now cited as being outside the realm of socially accepted norms. Today, its threat to one's health is known, but regardless of this knowledge, it is spreading rapidly. Although public awareness of bulimia started in the 1980's, it is sad to say that even in 2020, this "disorder" still exists, not only in our young women, and young men but also in **adults who have endured it since their teenage years.**

When exactly bulimia became a "disorder" is not known. Some of the earliest cases recorded today originated several years before it became a publicly announced issue. One case that I am aware of originated 60 years ago. This lady had begun to binge and purge in 1950. When her mother discovered that her daughter had been "ill" after certain meals, she sent her to several doctors, believing that I may have been the cause of allergies. No doctor could diagnose the problem as physical. It was not until 27 years later that it was discovered to have been a voluntary act that had eventually been planted into the subconscious, creating a belief in the mind of the bulimic that it was physical rather than psychological. Once this young lady finally came to terms with it by admitting that it was indeed a voluntary act, she was also able to come to terms with the hidden fear she had of gaining weight, which led to this behavior, but even more so, the psychological issues that were involved.

Another case that was recorded in the early 1980s revealed that a woman had suffered for 30 years from bulimia. It had not been until the latter three years that she was able to acquire help for her disorder. Her greatest concern was the fact that all the doctors she had visited in all the years of being bulimic, none had been able to diagnose the "disorder". She pleaded for better awareness.

Even with these earlier cases, it is still a mystery as to when bingeing and purging became a "disorder". What we do know is that in the last six decades, the frequency has been extensive enough to research, create public support, and for media coverage. Significant support started in the early 1980s and continues to grow in an attempt to eliminate the disorder as best possible.

The primary concerns about eating disorders originated with the increase of Anorexia Nervosa, a condition more easily detected as it involves self-starvation and a remarkable weight loss. Most of the studies conducted in the late nineteen seventies and early nineteen eighties were geared towards this particular disorder.

Bulimia, being harder to detect, was not as commonly researched until the late 1980s. Though weight loss often accompanies this disorder (though not always, as at times weight gain can be present), the extent of the loss is not as severe and the physical damages are not always as readily uncovered, as they take longer periods to appear. Bulimia, unlike anorexia nervosa's self-starvation, pertains to bingeing on large quantities of food (up to 10 to 20,000 calories) followed by self-induced vomiting, the use of laxatives, diuretics, or enemas. Recent studies now show bulimia to be more prevalent than anorexia. Overall, the increase in eating disorders in men and women is almost unequivocally correlated to the increased popularity of weight-loss diets in our society. Present-day estimates from the bulimia and Anorexia Nervosa Association – CAN/AM faculty of human kinetics, show that 15% to 30% of women and 5% to 10% of men are inflicted with some form of eating disorder, and the ages range from 7 to 70 years.

Bulimia is disconcerting. In writing this book, I am hoping that it can help others overcome this fear of reaching out and guide the bulimic to recover in the easiest possible way there could be if there is such a way. I cannot guarantee that the information provided will produce a sure cure. However, I can hope that it can. In the pages that follow, I have outlined several aspects of bulimia, as well as including my own experience. For those who are bulimic and have purchased this book, this is the first step towards recovery, as you have realized that you need help. All the best to you and here is hoping this is the book you have been waiting for. Good luck!!

Note: as the majority of sufferers are women, the bulimic will be referred to as she throughout this book, keeping in mind however that this is a disorder that does affect men as well.

"If I don't ask "Why me?" after my victories, I cannot ask "Why me?" after my setbacks and disasters"

Arthur Ashe

WHY ME

I don't know if you remember long ago as a child, how truly satisfied you had been with yourself, your achievements, your dreams, and your own image. I can. This came to pass however when, during my teenage years, the dieting craze was born. Being surrounded by friends who consistently claimed that they were fat (though they weren't) and shared their dieting schemes to correct their image, made it difficult not to get caught up in the rat race.

So, what has resulted from this craze? Well, in the 80s our drawers became cluttered with magazines and books on dieting and exercise. We have been granted a wide variety of choices of diets, anywhere from junk food diets; honey, oil, and vinegar diets; To the more popular grapefruit diets. And of course, to accompany these meager menus, we have been encouraged to join in on the recent fitness craze. You know the one I'm talking about. The one where you exercise and exercise and exercise just to look like Jane Fonda (who incidentally had been billed bulimic at one time as well). yes, exercise, exercise, and exercise, they tell us. Today it's all over the Internet.

Here is a picture of some of the celebrities that came out admitting their struggles with bulimia.

Before we know it, we are lost in a title wave of regimes and routines, strict as they are, trying eagerly to lose the extra 10 pounds that the weight charts tell us must be melted to attain our "ideal weight". I'm not sure that anyone can define an "ideal weight". Ideal for who? But it is society's measurements, and what society says goes. Forget the Marilyn Monroe look. That's out. Now it's the Twiggy look and you are encouraged to attain that bony figure as quickly as possible. This shouldn't pose any problems either, as you have thousands of books to guide you to it - even YouTube videos if you prefer visuals.

Let's face it. Few of us have been able to avoid the influence set upon us by peer pressure and the media. As an incentive in attaining the same skeletal forms as our idols, we have learned to paste or plaster the walls with pictures of emaciated models from magazines or save pictures to our cell phones. Some of us even place these on a refrigerator, hoping that they will somehow inhibit us from going beyond the door to where lies the sinful array of calories. To tell you the truth, not a locked door would have stopped me. When the urges came to binge, I had the strength of Mr. T and the incredible Hulk together. No obstacles were too big.

Inevitably, however, a revelation is realized. The sad part about dieting is that it is not as easy as it appears on the papers of a diet book or online. Instagram and Facebook have been cited as contributing to eating disorders, including bulimia. Hollywood has made many references to bulimia in shows and movies, mocking it, and making a joke of it. Although I chuckle, in the way one would laugh at themselves, I also find it interesting that if one mocks someone who has a "mental health issue" it is perceived as distasteful. Bulimia is a mental health issue, hence I believe it to be inappropriate.

Seemingly common for many of us, the more we tried to follow the restrictive diets, the more we crave the foods we deny ourselves.

Now, why does this happen? A couple of reasons this happens because the lack of nutrients provided to the body has set off a signal to our brain, warning it of the insufficient quantity of nourishment provided for proper functioning. Often the result leads to wild binges. These binges, in turn, disrupt the ability to tap into our hunger awareness and control signals. Because we are too busy eating at high speed, we surpassed the red light warning us that it is time to stop. The consequence of all this is a feeling of lost control which reverses the initial intent of dieting. In other words, weight is not decreased but increased. As the scales tip the wrong way and the inability to follow strict diets becomes reality, a seed is planted. It is the seed of panic. This thing grows, and the feeling of being entangled in a growing vine of weight creates the desire to search for a way to break loose. For some of us, this frenzy develops into an eating disorder. Some, like me, chose bulimia as the ultimate escape. Easily concealed, it seems the ultimate solution - contrary to the adage - of "how to having your cake and eat it all too". But ...

The obsession with food, calories, and weight persists even through this transformation from dieting to bulimia. The damage to the physical and psychological functions increases through more severe degrees of self-abuse and lack of nutrition.

In my interviews with bulimics, a majority admitted that dieting produced feelings of dissatisfaction with their self-image, caused them to put on weight through lack of willpower, and disrupted their ability to know when they were full.

Once bulimia set in, these women found that they had a more difficult time coping with feelings of depression. They, as I, began to perceive everyday problems as less tolerable than usual. Fears began to arise. Fear of growing older, of responsibility, of letting go of childhood beliefs, of being incompetent. Yet all the while, they wanted to be treated as adults, let go of the hold of others they felt were controlling their lives. They wanted to do things for themselves rather than others but felt unable to because they did not like themselves enough anymore to bother. All these common thoughts are the disorder. To assume the opposite, that the fears and feelings of helplessness are the cause, can be hazardous. These hazards are used as excuses, as a crutch, recovery can become much more difficult. Those who perceive depression as the cause of bulimia consequently feel that it is only when they have resolved those problems that bulimia will be cured. Yet it is a known fact that dwelling on depression only serves to worsen the condition, producing deeper depths of self-pity, low self-esteem, anxiety, fears, moodiness, sluggishness, and even isolation from others. Therefore to hold to the belief that depression is the route to bulimia is a defeating perception that can only serve to threaten the process of recovery. On the other hand, as long as you can perceive the emotions as consequence rather than a cause of bulimia, you're allowing the doors to other possibilities to open.

So now you ask why me? Well, it is you and I because we got caught up in the dieting craze, the wish to be slim, conform to society's measurements.

Bulimia was once believed to be a disorder that primarily affected women in the middle to upper class, but it is now found to affect most anyone, from any class in any age group. Many bulimics are, however, known to have a history of being overachievers, perfectionists, and not only fear but refuse to accept failure. Also, many become believers of the disillusion that thinness is a symbol of success, beauty, and happiness. From this, these men and women feel that being overweight could jeopardize job opportunities, career advancement, a personal relationship with the opposite sex. Body image, as a result, becomes a major concern, at times reaching the highest level of priority.

Hopefully, soon (which should have been years ago really), we will come to see a more prominent shift towards acceptance of realistic body images, as well as a lowered frequency of published diets, leading young girls and women towards a better understanding that we were not meant to have protruding bones. Women are women, men are men, not stick figures, and our shape was created for a purpose not to be overlooked. For women, I can only hope that the hourglass will be ours again. Until then we will have to look at other solutions to the problem.

In the interim, instead of looking out, we have to look inside ourselves. We must celebrate our victories, not our setbacks, no matter how small. We must turn the "why me?" which focuses on the negative and turn the "why me?" to the positive. It will give a whole new perspective to our lives.

"While sitting in the quicksand we've created, we have two choices to make. Let ourselves sink or reach out to the many hands of true friends offering us help to get out."

LaurieAnn

THE DISCOVERY

I, like many, know the surge of emotions that arise when someone discovers you are bulimic. The feelings of hate and betrayal are not just delusions, they are very real and very frightening. The extent of these feelings has no bearing on who it is that approaches you with the news that they have become aware of the secret. Be it friend, parent, or sibling, or even doctor, the hatred of the discovery is equally as strong.

Some of us who have been discovered have experienced what it is like to be bombarded with harsh negativity. Retorts have been known to range from being threatened to be thrown out of on the street, to accusations of being self-destructive at the expense of others, to being questions as to whether we expected others to pay the hospital bill when the time came to be admitted. This approach is wrong, but not uncommon. When I was first confronted with the issue, it was devastating. Not only had my secret been exposed, but my being had been tortured as well. I became good for nothing, a bright young girl gone bad and an embarrassment. In effect, I was a social failure.

My counter-reaction was one of silence. I'm not sure if it was to avoid any admittance, or simply because I had nothing to say. I do know that after it was all over a sickly thought of satisfaction skimmed through my mind. I had recurring visions of my parents standing there in all their grand authority, having no control over what I was doing. For once in my life, I had control. It was my body and

there was nothing they could do to force me to live by their wishes. All the energy inputted in the scolding was useless in exerting any influence on the arrest of my behavior.

My poor parents. They knew nothing of the disorder at that time. They chided, then let it go. Silence, in effect, became their only way of dealing with it.

Many of us who share the experience of having BEEN subjected to reproach have more than likely been the victims of the uninformed. Today, after 30 years of awareness it's astounding how many people still don't' know about bulimia. What must be realized in this case, is that ignorance creates fear. Parents facing the first-time experience of not being able to control their child become despondent through their feelings of helplessness. In themselves, they begin to ask where they failed. The lack of communication present under these circumstances pushes the two parties to opposite ends of a tunnel. Each side, engrossed in their self-interests, lose sight of the proper actions to take in meeting halfway. Irrational behavior obstructs the path of coming together. But for the sake of recovery, the ultimate answer is to meet each other in the middle and guide one another out of the dark.

My parents, having granted me no support delayed my decision

to get help. Yet I can't stress enough how important it is not to let this sort of discouragement from others affect your decision to get well, as it had with me. Most of the time words, or even silence, evolve from irrational thoughts and are not meant to be hurtful. When you let the negative influence you, you are only hurting yourself. Always remember that most of the time those who approach you with the issue are unaware of the aspects of bulimia. Their ignorance is the root of the negative reactions, be they verbal or silent, but it is not to say no care is involved. There is just no conception present of how the matter should be dealt with. Whatever the case, never forget that it takes courage to face someone on a sensitive issue, but it also takes concern, even if it isn't always apparent.

If those who approach you are not willing to be supportive, as it was in my case, you may travel a lonely road and a frightening one unless you decide to take the action yourself. In the case where you feel there may be repercussions or denial of assistance, I advise that discussion on the subject be avoided, as it may only give rise to a dispute. Instead, get outside help at your discretion when you feel the necessity to share your anguish with someone who will understand and be able to help. What you are doing, in essence, is avoiding negative feedback or drawback from your being bulimic and searching for someone who will provide you with positive feelings, support, and encouragement to get well.

In the meantime, try not to let self-indulgence in your problems blind you of the worry of others, nor the fears that they are most probably hiding behind the shield of authority and negative discipline. Remember, they are concealing their anxieties, much as you are, but from a different perspective. In the end remember, it is not them, but you who will choose what to do about your life.

"Disruption isn't what happens to you, it's about how you respond to what happens to you."

Jay Samit

DISRUPTION

When bulimia advances into the stage of being an obsession, it is finely engraved in your mind and is proceeding to create a certain degree of emotional instability. In essence, the obsession that has settled in your subconscious, and your conscious mind struggles with that alien within, what I refer to as an ID. This ID is what disrupts your habitual feeling and drives you to social isolation, often to give yourself the freedom to binge whenever the urge arises. My ID kept me from being with friends for days on end to allow for this peace. But peace is not the ultimate acquisition in these instances. The hidden behavior patterns eventually give rise to bouts of guilt and feelings of abnormality, not to mention fatigue from excessive purging.

Disruptions in my social life went even further. The longer I was bulimic, the greater my fear of social gatherings that included dining. Silly thoughts would cluster in my mind, such as "would I find a way to eat then purge without any suspicions arising from others? Could I control the amount of food I ate? With the toilet flush properly?" These were, as anyone could see, thoughts that were not general by nature. They were the thoughts of my ID that

gnawing at my concentration and wemt as far as ruining an evening that could well have been enjoyed if bulimia had not been present.

My ID also became the mother of hate, hate directed towards anyone who interrupted bingeing, or towards those responsible for requesting my attendance at functions that included food. I hated these people like I never hated before. The frightening thing is that "these people" were usually friends or relatives. Those people dearest to me. In becoming a different person, I disliked anyone's presence when urges to eat arose, angered by the fact that they were intruding and refusing me the opportunity to fill my void, to allow me privacy and solitude to do what I wanted to do. And the more I hated them, the more I hated myself for it.

DISRUPTION

It didn't end there. In time I began to crawl into myself and deny myself the chance to build emotional ties to anyone. I didn't want to love, and I surely didn't want anyone to love me. I just wanted to be left alone. This lack of desire for human interaction, however, drove loneliness to live with me, accompanied by self-pity and depression. All these blinded me from the reality of the dreaded circle I was living in.

Then one day, after the world had been shut out, I realized that I was truly alone. Suddenly bulimia seemed like my only friend. I held on to it, afraid that if I let it go, I would no longer have anything to live for. I felt it was all I had left. Yeah, what I was ultimately admitting is that my only friend was a distraction, and ultimately the forfeit of my life.

Doctor Leo Buscaglia, the author of Living, Loving and Learning, wrote that "we revel in denying ourselves. It seems a self-punishment kind of thing." In effect, this is what bulimia is. It is a denial of growth, of human interaction, of facing our true self. It is the cruelest punishment and one that is self-inflicted. We are afraid to show others who we truly are and believe that by creating a shield no one will ever see how truly fallible we are. But it is this shield that eventually closes in on us and traps us in a tiny corner with food as our only means for comfort. And thus, we stunt our growth. We lie hidden behind our secret and become sightless to the wonders that exist beyond our world.

The only way to regain this growth and ability to recognize the beauty of life is by facing that perceived "fallible" self and realizing that it isn't as bad as we think because really, it isn't. Learn to accept this and you will learn to believe it. Ultimately, it is how you wish to see yourself that will become the reflection you have of yourself.

Let's face it. The truth is bulimia is not the only friend you have. Bulimia is not a friend at all. It was you who chose to see it as such, hence only you can choose to reassess this and realize the deceit in this belief.

While sitting in the quicksand we've created, we have two choices to make. Let ourselves sink or reach out to the many hands of true friends offering us help to get out. You can bet too that they are there. Though we become blind to the many faces that are hoping for our recovery or are willing to support us through it, we eventually must regain sight and realize they are still there and always have been. Reach out! You may be surprised at who's hand is most eager to pull you out and who's ears are most eager to listen.

"You will never find yourself until you face the truth"

Pearl Bailey

FACING THE TRUTH

So, what route does one take towards recovery? Well, the first one is the route of admission. Before going any further and trying to correct the problem, we must first confront the fact that indeed being bulimic means you have a problem. It is like the person who drinks too must first admit he or she is an alcoholic. This, however simple it may appear in writing, is not so simple in the psychological sense. The last thing anyone wants to do is to admit that they are doing something wrong. This difficulty of admitting our faults originates from our egos. The ego is something we are born with. As a child, it is what produces the desire to be our own person with our own right, with personal needs and thoughts. It is, in other words, our desire to be unique and to know this.

Later, however, the ego becomes confused and the world injects us with the belief that happiness is directly related to getting what we want and to the fulfillment of our desires.

Bulimia seeks control of the ego. It acts on our fear of gaining weight and transforms it into a need to control it. To admit that we are doing this in unethical ways and a threat to our wellbeing then becomes difficult. This is because we falsely believe that we have found the solution to the desire to control our weight and thus have satisfied our pseudo ego's need.

To regain a proper knowledge of what our true desires are, we must retract the ego from the control of bulimia and position it under our self-control. To do this we must come to terms with the fact that bulimia is a negative force in our lives. We must be aware of the social and personal disruptions it is responsible for. We must know that bulimia has been the enemy that has been keeping us from the happiness we deserve. Happiness is derived from living. If we do not realize this and choose to hold on to our false needs and the unethical ways of fulfilling this need, everything else in our life becomes secondary. We then build the cage which locks us away from the rest of our hopes and wishes.

And choosing to grasp the reality that bulimia is disrupting your existence, you can continue to the next evaluation - that of your negative attitudes. Dr. Buscaglia, who offered me such inspiration through his work, and continues today, wrote that "you are nothing if you think you are nothing ". He believed that the greatest threat to the fulfillment of ourselves is the "self-defeating self ". It is a part of us that creates images of ourselves without anything to back it up. The danger in bulimia is that when you can't explain the reasons for its existence, it may well add to your feeling of inadequacy. To cover up these feelings, you turn to excuses for the behavior.

If we wish to go forth to recovery, we must begin by leaving these excuses aside and step forward towards taking on responsibility for our condition. This is not saying that the fault is all ours that the whole situation arose, but it is realizing that we are the only ones who can take responsibility for it in any circumstance. We, not anyone else, must directly deal with the disorder, therefore we, not anyone else, must own up to it.

What am I saying? I'm saying to stop blaming others. It is so easy to find a scapegoat to relieve us of our guilt. It may well be that the scapegoat did, in fact, contribute to our bulimia, but we are the ones who let it affect us in the way we have and we are the ones who must learn to reverse the effects and take control.

The other thing I am saying is to stop believing that food is a "comfort" treatment. By now we are well aware that it has never solved any of our problems. If anything, it has only added to them. Food fails greatly in its ability to appease the hurt and therefore must be broken from its link to our emotions. Food is fuel for thought and health, and though it has a social inclination to it, it can still be enjoyed in reasonable quantities. Perhaps even more so than in excess. It cannot, however, fill an emotional void.

Bulimia is not a proper shield for failure. To use it as such is a disillusionment of reality. It also closes the doors to other ways of facing fears productively.

As the adage saying goes, bulimia is in effect a "wolf in sheep's clothing". First believed to be the ultimate solution to the diet struggle, then believed to be the ultimate solution to relieving anxieties and to shield the true abuse of food and eventually our true self, it is, in reality, false security leading to self-sabotage, self-defeat, and self-destruction.

When you can admit you have a problem when you can let go of all the excuses for it fed to you by books and literature on the subject, then you can open up to other possibilities, and when you can come forward and admit that you are not quite sure where it all began - When you can let go of the blame and look to other means of dealing with it - then you are facing up to it. And when this comes to be, you will most likely find that you will feel stronger and more able to proceed towards recovery. In other words, you are building yourself up for a battle you will ultimately win.

"What You Are Looking For Is Not Out There, It's In YOU"

Anonymous

FACING THE SELF

So, you have faced the truth that bulimia is a problem, and that's one thing. Now you must face yourself. What I mean by this is that you must look at the image you have of yourself.

Bulimia has tarnished many positive perceptions of your true being. Depression has caused you to dwell on your shortcomings, your failures in personal endeavors, your deficiency, and character, your inability to cope with certain factors. Through these negative attitudes you may have come to see yourself as a good for nothing, a person molded into something you are not, a mass amongst the mass, a deceitful liar through your attempts to conceal your problem.

Many faults such as feeling like a klutz, unable to express yourself properly, lacking coordination, all become magnified, seeming 1000 times greater than they are. You may even categorize yourself under such headings as a dummy, inefficient, or scatterbrain. You may even use this "toxic vocabulary" in the words you speak to yourself. Never once do you stop to realize that others just don't have that same perception of you. You believe they do because you do. You, yourself, build the false beliefs of how others see you.

Stop for a moment. Look inside yourself. Sit down and take a pen at hand and on a piece of paper, no matter how hard it seems, write down what you think is good about yourself.

The first time I did this exercise I must have sat for 15 to 30 minutes before I could think of one thing. Once I did find that one thing, it was followed by another and another. The characteristics were quite simple, but they were, in all their simplicity, good. Things like loving others, wanting to help others, trying to understand both sides of an argument, giving others the benefit of the doubt. Suddenly I was writing my own beliefs of what was good, such as being emotional, sensitive, sentimental. These were characteristics others might debate on whether they are virtues or vices. To me, however, they were unquestionably virtues and so I wrote these down. It no longer mattered what others thought. What I liked was what I wrote. So, I gathered all these little notes about the good and with a few of the bad added and proceeded to write a poem. It went like this:

> *Time*
>
> *Time to think, to ponder, to feel emotion.*
> *Not all positive.*
> *I would often like to believe they can be.*
> *I am sure they can, someday.*
>
> *Pain. Loneliness.*
> *Do you ever feel them?*
> *Do you ever speak to them?*
> *I feel them. I couldn't speak them,*
> *Because I didn't understand them.*
> *Bury them. Must be happy. Always.*
> *Silence the pain. All trivial.*
> *No one will understand. Being silly.*
> *Forget them someplace.*
>
> *Sometimes they surface though.*
> *By then I can't identify them all.*
> *So, I cry, not knowing why.*
>
> *What pain could I possibly have?*
> *Me?*
> *Anxieties locked inside. Building pressure.*
> *No communication, no escape*

*It's not easy to speak when silence has been a
Friend.*

*What do I want?
To be happy. To know me. Who am I? LaurieAnn.
But who is she?*

*The child who longs for attention and affection?
Or the loner, needing time, solitude.
Or both.*

*What is being happy?
Is it having a loyal, honest, open friendship?
Is it being independent?
Is it being there for those I love,
Or is it my needing them to be there?
Or even worse, is it needing me.*

*What am I looking for?
Is it sensitivity, sentimentality, loyalty?
Is it walking through the park?
Sharing the loves of life?
Collecting seashells, petals from wildflowers,
Nature's gifts?
Is it sharing the pain and joys
I experience when I am alone?
With another?
Is it idealistic?
Perhaps.*

*What is love?
Is it being independent?
Or does love mean dependency, to a point,
On another?*

Maybe I don't know.

Nothing is perfect.
No one is perfect.
No one comes near to perfection.
I must know this.
I must be better than perfect,
I must be human and learn to accept failure.

What is my direction?
Sometimes I fear not knowing.
Changes. They're frightening.

I can't go on hiding the real me.
I can't go on molding myself into
What others want.
I need to be me.

My pain was not admitting to myself
Nor anyone else, who I am.
Fear of losing respect if they saw the real me.
LaurieAnn.
The idealistic one.
The one who finds it hard to deal
With some of life's stressful situations,
 Who then needs someone to lean on?
Someone to listen and not make me feel that my
Fears are silly.

Emotional, sensitive, sentimental.
Me.

Justice.
What justice is there in telling someone

They are wrong to be themselves?
To let their feelings flow?
Their human flaws to show?

Extremes.
High then low.
Happy then depressed.
Abundant love, no love.
Then I must find a medium.
I shall because I long to.

Have you ever felt as though you've
Never loved at all?
That it was only conditional?
That perhaps you could live without anyone?
I have.
At my most vulnerable times, I have.
I confuse my lack of emotion with the inability
To deal with them.
I turned them off. It's easy. Not efficient.

I need to teach myself things I never knew before.
I need to learn about myself.
But learning takes time

I still wander too far to one extreme at times.
In time I will have it together.
Time.

But it cannot change me.
Not all of me.
Not the me who needs to let out the hurt,
Sorrow, no matter how trivial it seems.
Sensitivity.

It cannot change the me who can love.
Who wants to love.
Who wants to learn even more about loving me.
Who wants to share that me.

I hold the compass,
I must point the direction I longed to take
Then follow it.

I'm a stray,
For I fall short of expectations at times,
Because I am human.
I wouldn't want to be anything else though.
Nor anyone else.

Though at the time I wrote this poem I still had bulimia, it showed me that even with my degree of low self-esteem, I did still have some high esteem buried somewhere and it was that bit that was to be watered and cared for to eventually blossom and become a centerpiece in my mind with such beauty sitting in the middle, the beauty of finally seeing the good I possessed and dwelling on that rather than the bad. The rest became less important to focus on.

Hopefully, through this exercise, you can come to see the spot inside which still holds that bit of belief in yourself and learn to focus on it. These traits that you list are the basis for the creation of a better mental image of your true self.

Now I realize that it is not an easy thing to do. After all, many of us have focused on negativity for quite some time. But now it's time to change that. You must realize that you are worth something. No one on earth isn't. To enforce this belief, you must see your good values. The first one is obvious - you are alive.

If you are finding that you are unable to begin your list, I would recommend that you read Dr. Leo Buscaglia's book *Living, Loving and Learning*, which was mentioned earlier. In it, Dr. Buscaglia discussed the value of humanity and the value of the self. Also recommended is his book called Loving Each Other. These may help you to see these positive traits I speak of.

All in all, this exercise may well be the discovery of what you have been missing in your life. You will likely find that it is you that has been missing. In the maze of negative emotions, it is possible, and highly likely, that you have lost yourself. Your list may guide you back to that self. I can only hope it does, as it did for me.

I'm not going to lie. Fighting bulimia is not easy. But with even the slightest belief in yourself, it can make the struggle more bearable, because when you believe in yourself, you can believe in your ability to do what you want to do, for you, and that you are the one who controls your destiny. When you believe in yourself, you can believe that anything is possible. It is also your key to reality.

Remember:

"If you can dream it, you can achieve it,
If you can imagine it, you can become it. "
Author unknown

I also found this chart that follows to be helpful. Take a pen a paper and you can also start with this. It will give you great insight.

20 DAY STEPS

1. My best personality trait is,	11. I am valuable,
2. I am proud of myself because,	12. I am confident when,
3. I am excited for,	13. I am skilful in,
4. My strengths are,	14. My favorite inspiring quote is,
5. I love my,	15. 3 things I love about myself are,
6. My favorite memory is,	16. 5 positive things about me are,
7. I laugh most when,	17. My insecurities make me me,
8. My goal in life is,	18. What motivates me is,
9. A note for my future self is,	19. I have great energy,
10. I am worth it because,	20. I love myself!

"Sometimes the smallest step in the right direction ends up being the biggest step of your life. Tiptoe if you must, but take the step."

Author Unknown

STEP BY STEP

So, you've come this far into the book. I do hope this means that you have decided to continue and be serious about stepping forth towards recovery. As with most things, however, there is not, to my knowledge, just one way to recover which is suitable for everyone. The one I outlined in this book however is the one that I greatly believed to be the most efficient.

Before you start, you must be in the right frame of mind. This means that you must have followed the guidelines of the previous chapters of taking responsibility for your disorder. With this acquisition, you can then progress towards working on that responsibility. To follow through, you must then commit to correcting the disorder. In other words, you are committing yourself, with kindness, love, and understanding.

The next objective is to clear the mental path from any previous negative beliefs. This will prepare you for new positive insights. So, relax and free yourself and others of any blame to allow for the maintenance of a clear perspective. Your willingness to change rather than to blame is going to be a big factor in the ultimate success of the task at hand.

In the previous chapter, I wrote in my poem about the emotions I needed to deal with outwardly to face up to myself. This must also be true for you. We all must be able to acknowledge our emotions and express them without inhibitions. This absolves guilt and helps in comprehending ourselves better.

Allow others to love you. Love feeds into the positive transmission of the brain. Overcoming the fear of loving and being loved can help you. Yes, love makes us vulnerable at times, but vulnerability is a small price to pay for the wonder that adds to the greatness of being human. This may not fall under your perception of perfection, but it is this step over the boundaries of perfection into the boundaries of imperfection that makes us human and it is this humanity that unites everyone. It is this imperfection that allows us to understand one another better. Not many of us can relate to flawlessness because none of us are flawless.

But being human is not only being less than perfect. It is also enriched with very precious qualities, one of them being forgiveness. This power of forgiveness can be used to open doors to acceptance of both others and ourselves. It creates a passage to learning. Learning from pain, then releasing it, or learning from joy and carrying on. Dr. Buscaglia has a powerful passage which states:

"We go around pretending that we have it all together, that we are so secure, that we don't need when it would be much easier to be able to say 'I'm vulnerable, I make mistakes. I'm imperfect. I'm afraid. In other words, I'm a human being. And that's my greatest asset. That's all I want to be '."

That is all you should want to be, for that is what you are. You can't be perfect. No one can. So, remove all the unrealistic goals and start building ones within your ability. In terms of bulimia, this means allotting reasonable time goals for your recovery. Understanding that it does not take a day is important. Time. Allow for it.

So now we're going to take it "step by step". The first of these is the step towards arresting the denial process. Stop denying yourself things. Where food is concerned, try to stop categorizing it into "fat" or "skinny" foods. By denying yourself the right to having something you desire, like food in the "fat "category, you are only creating a mental focus on it. Do you want a chocolate chip cookie? Then have one. Believe me, you aren't going to gain that 10 pounds you believe you will.

Now, if you are thinking what I think you are thinking, think again. You don't believe that you can stop at 1, right? Well, that is because you have placed this belief in your mind. Now tell yourself that you can. You may be surprised. Anything you tell yourself you can do, you can.

By removing the restriction on the foods, you can and cannot eat, you are also removing much of the strains towards achieving good eating habits. Being able to have what you want will likely rid you of the urge to binge. The reason for this is that for the most part, binges consist of foods that are not usually perceived as acceptable in trying to remain thin. Often, we concentrate on our urges to have these forbidden foods to the point where we can no longer stand the minds lure into having it. If, however, we tell ourselves that we can have them if we want them, our minds are less likely to dwell on the desire. This attitude is very much like one we often possess as children. "If I can't have it, then I want it!" So say you can have it, and you will probably find that you don't want it as much anymore.

When you learn to remove false beliefs in realizing that one or two cookies are not going to put 2 inches onto your hips, you will feel less threatened by them. By lowering this threat, you can increase your ability to face such prohibited foods with more confidence and less fear. As you learn to do this, you will learn how to eat these foods in correct portions. Remember, no proper quantity of food will threaten your body weight.

Again, I know all this is much easier written than done, but the whole point here is to believe that it can be done, and it will.

To complete a better outlook on food, free it of the correlation to it as a treat or reward. A treat or reward is something you associate with the recompense for having been good. Well, if you want rewards, then try buying yourself a book, or something that genuinely interests you. Food is not a virtuous reward. It is however a necessity for health and survival (and can be enjoyed at the same time in time, as it once was). It is the fruit of life and should be enjoyed for its ability to induce a better feeling with its nutrients which feed the body and the brain. Hard to do, right? After all, food has been used for emotional suffocations and has become associated with this process. This is what must end. Food must be disengaged from this association in your mind and become something other than an emotional type. It must be understood for what it is - your lifeline.

An especially important body mechanism perceived to be lost when one becomes bulimic is the one that warns you when you are full.

I, however, believe that this is not lost, but merely ignored and like many things, when ignored for long enough, it falls to the background and is temporarily forgotten. But you can bring it forth again. You can do this by paying attention to it. If you begin to tell yourself that you have use for it again, it will likely be remembered and once again become your guide.

In my own experience of wishing my hunger and fullness signals to reawaken, I began by eating small portions of food whenever my stomach seemed to feel the need for it. I mean "really" feel the need for it. This takes place when there is a sort of hollow ache which is often accompanied by rumbles. By eating slowly, it helped me reach the point of satisfaction without reaching the feeling of "uncomfortable fullness" that used to be associated with the subsequent feeling of guilt which led to bingeing and purging.

A certain awareness was born from this. The awareness of craving foods when no hollow aching feeling was present. When this situation arose, I knew that my desires for food were caused by emotions rather than by hunger. At first, I almost fell prey to these desires, but all the while I tried to figure out the connection. How was I feeling at the time? Sometimes I didn't know. My cravings overpowered my ability to think straight and logically. All I wanted was food. I didn't care about anything else. But after a while, the connection comes to light. And with this came the ability to decipher between true hunger and pseudo hunger.

Once I became more familiar with hunger and satisfaction, I realized just how wonderful this mechanism was. It didn't only tell me when to eat and went to stop, it was also dependable. That is, it became my most treasured guide as to how much food my body needed to operate at its best and maintain its proper weight. By abiding by the signals, I no longer had to worry about calories, and eventually, I let go of my obsession with the fear of gaining weight.

If you can achieve the same ability to reawaken your signal mechanism which tells you when you feel you have had enough, or warn you that you require more, you will realize the worth of it. This signal is the secret to maintaining your health at its best and stabilizing the weight at which you should be to function at your best. Now all this is going to take time. The idea here is to concentrate and tap into your body functions. Being aware of them is the best first step towards this. When you know it exists, you can better control the process of re-establishing it in your mind and resituating it in your daily awareness patterns.

The next objective we must undertake in the recovery process is that of decreasing the binges. To do this, you must accept the fact that you might and probably will purge again. This is fine. As I said before, you cannot succeed if you take on the attitude "this binge will be my last ". By saying this, you are simply creating unrealistic goals for yourself, and the next time you do binge, you will feel guilt. Guilt, by the way, is one of the most wicked obstructors of confidence towards recovering. So, rid yourself of misconceptions that you can do it in one day or one week. Be patient. It's important.

If you succumb to urges to eat, learn to tell yourself that this is okay. There is always tomorrow to try again to do better. Don't bother blaming your binge on anyone or anything either. You did it. Fine. Now forget it. By placing blame on others or yourself, you are simply opening yourself up to defeat. Again, you did it. Okay. Now forget it.

The most crucial point in the step-by-step procedure towards recovery is to not force it or rush it. Tell yourself you will try to (never say you will) do better than before. Trying is the secret because it does not place restrictive demands on you. You must want to do something. This is the route to reaching the ultimate goal.

Remember,

"If you want to be anything you want to be, you can be it - provided you're willing to get your fingers dirty, willing to suffer a little bit, willing to struggle a little bit because it doesn't come naturally. "

Leo Buscaglia

But most of all, you must **want** to.

During my recovery, I found that monitoring my bingeing was quite helpful. I don't mean the kind of monitoring that some psychiatrists want you to do. The first psychiatrist I went to see wanted me to monitor everything I ate, when I ate it, where I ate it, how I ate it, how I felt when I ate it and how I felt after eating and after vomiting. This, to say the least, was exhausting, and usually the last thing I wanted to do before or after eating. Worse yet, usually, when I binged, I was not aware of everything I ate common or how I was feeling. Food was a way to conceal my true feelings and had come to do this quite well. So, for myself, I simply wrote down the time I had eaten. If I kept it in, I would write down when it was I ate. If I did binge then purge, I simply wrote BP next to the time I had done it. In essence, what this monitoring did for me was to give me a rough idea of what time I was most vulnerable to bingeing. After a while, I even notice that there were certain times during that day that seemed to trigger the urge. There was a distinguishable pattern in my eating behavior.

When I first started recording this in my earlier stages of bulimia, the data showed that breakfast, which was usually consumed before 8:00 in the morning and was composed of highly nutritious foods, usually remained within. However, vulnerable times for bingeing were 11 in the morning, lunchtime, 3:00 PM, 7:00 PM, and if I was up late, midnight to 1:00 AM. Strangely enough, I did not require any monitoring of feelings to eventually understand the pattern.

The pattern that emerged was related to certain states of mind. One of the most common is boredom, which today I realize was apathy. Bingeing was being used as a tool to allow time to pass more rapidly. By concentrating on eating and having something to do, hours no longer felt like days, but rather minutes.

The next thing I had to do then was to assess why it was I was bored (or rather apathetic). This did not need much effort. I had long since become aware of the dissatisfaction I had with my job, and it was this dissatisfaction that made for the day drag on unbearably.

In the evening, my "boredom" was aggravated by the lack of external activities in my life. Much time was spent simply sitting in front of the television. Eating was one way to keep my hands and mouth occupied all the while allowing me to continue viewing the programs. Boredom/apathy was not the only state that triggered the binges. Fatigue was another trigger of late-night binges. This sluggishness was not necessarily reserved for evenings though. The same vulnerability also occurred during the days which followed sleepless nights or the shortage of time allotted to sleep. The frightening thing about this was that the more I binged, the lower my energy became, and the greater my susceptibility to bingeing again. Subsequently, this was made for multiple bingeing and purging sessions within a day. It was a vicious and exhausting circle.

There is still one more reason why our resistance to bingeing is lowered. This is not a state so much as it is a factor. I am talking here about the use of drugs or alcohol. I'm not a drug user, but I have had periods of drinking more than I should, and I've found that each time I did my control level fell and I lost my ability to overcome my urges to eat.

Depression, anger, and sorrow, what I call emotional states, also create desires to binge. I also believe that if the focus primarily on removing boredom/apathy and implementing healthy eating, depression will most likely be lessened substantially, as will anger and sorrow.

(As far as alcohol and drug use goes, these should be avoided. Be aware of their effects on your mind concerning control may be sufficient motivation for you to choose to stay away from them.)

Aside from the above, there is also a physical condition that can trigger binges. This is the condition of feeling that the quantity of food consumed was too great. Often when we, as bulimics, feel a fullness or perceive our stomachs to protrude slightly, we panic. We tend to relate this to having eaten too much and assume the result may contribute to the weight gain. It is advised therefore that, as mentioned before, food should be eaten slowly and concentration should be directed towards the feelings of your body.

If you choose to record what you eat and the results after the consumption, I would advise you to try to be aware of the times when you are either bored, tired, have felt discomfort after eating or consumed alcohol or taken drugs. I'm sure that you will find that a great many times, one of the above will have contributed to your urge. I also advise that your state of mind be your initial concern, as I said before, as once you work on these, you're likely going to be working on your emotions as well.

In the case where it appears that you cannot note anything but emotions, try to write down alternate ways of dealing with these. For instance, in the case of anger, instead of eating, you may want to go into your room and punch a pillow. Or perhaps more constructive, you may want to take a walk, which can help in straightening out your feelings. If you have a car, try taking a drive in the countryside. I have found this to be a valuable therapy in sorting out my thoughts.

For sorrow or disappointment, you may want to find a place where you can cry alone. Release those feelings if you must. Crying is not bad. It relieves a lot of the built-up anguish inside. Or perhaps you may want to write a poem or a letter describing why it is you believe you are sad. Try to write down how you could resolve this in ways other than with food. Will talking about it help? Then try to find someone to listen to you.

Once you become aware of the patterns of your eating behaviors and define possible alternatives to the situation, it is time to start working on these alternatives. For me, the dissatisfaction with my job was the first thing that had to be dealt with. To do this, I knew the only solution was to find another one. The prospect of leaving a secure job was frightening. But I knew that if I didn't do this, I would just continue to destroy myself. I was finally hired by a wonderful company in an office with a view. (I faced a wall in the other location). The atmosphere allowed me to go home in a state of accomplishment rather than frustration. This in turn affected my home life, where I began to enjoy greater peace of mind, free of lingering problems from my job.

My eating habits began to improve substantially after the move, but I still struggled with my mid-afternoon, which usually brought on a bout of fatigue. To resolve this, I told myself that bingeing was not going to take away the sluggishness, but only add to it and create further desires to eat later in the day. As such, I set this time aside to have a snack, which often helped in restoring my energy. The snack was anything from fruit to a cookie to a muffin. Whatever pleased me at the time. I believe that I could stop at one and I did. And as the days passed, this became easier and easier. There were even days where I would not even need the snack anymore and wouldn't even think about it.

Though my job was going well, and I soon ceased bingeing during daytime hours altogether, it was not over yet. I still had the

evenings to face. I knew very well why this created difficulty in control over my binges. It was because of the lack of things I had to do and the attachment that had grown into my greatest enemy of all - television. TV had long since become related to snacking binges, and it was not an easy habit to break. I realized then that I had to find alternatives. I sat down one night and wrote out a list. From this list, I chose the activities which appealed to me the most. The first of these was enrolling for courses through correspondence. I knew my attitude towards commitment and my preference to do things at my leisure. This is why I chose home studies. And as I always wanted to write well, I found journalism to be the most suitable choice. The course also added other hobbies to my daily life. I began to write more frequently in my spare time when homework was either completed or when I felt I needed a rest from it. When I didn't feel like doing either of these, I began to work on my drawings. I created a cartoon character and started my very own comic strip. It came to pass that every evening presented a new project which I love doing and as I love to do it, time passed by at an enjoyable speed.

With the added interest in my life, my binges gradually began to diminish on their own. Even when the urge did arise, I was beginning to be able to talk myself out of it. I would assess in my mind the feelings I would have after benching compared to those I would have if I turned to an alternative. I knew the latter would win. With the eventual process of allowing more and more meals per day to stay down, my mentality improved tremendously, and this added to the control I began to have over my urges. With each victory came a greater desire to continue. With each victory came a better feeling of health which was one of the greatest motivations. With each victory, I grew to love myself more, and consequently, love others more as well.

For many, the circumstances will differ. But what I am demonstrating here is the power of alternatives. Alternatives to eating as a means of dealing with certain states or emotions. These often proved to be much more rewarding and productive. For myself, the substitution meant receiving a diploma in Honors Journalism, sufficient comic strips to present to syndications, letters of reply from the Mayor, and the Prime Minister's office, many poems I enjoyed reading to myself, and a book manuscript.

From the time I began using my alternatives to eating, it took me four months to completely stop the binge/purge syndrome. I began with trying to make it through just one day. Every day I told myself the same thing. "Today I'm going to try to restrain from bingeing." The frequency of my binge-free days slowly increased from one day a week to three, to five, then finally to seven. What I was doing was transforming my practice of using alternatives into a habit. Once this implementation was achieved, I was able to let go of the use of food as a way to deal with emotions altogether.

Now though it took me four months from the time my alternatives were chosen to overcome bulimia, I must assure you that the process of recovery lasted one whole year. It took time for me to realize why I was bingeing, what to do about it, and finally to put these solutions to use. For some of you, the process may only take three months, for others yet, over a year. But as long as you are trying, the decrease of bingeing will materialize, and recovery will eventually be the ultimate reward.

The success alternatives presented led me to a great appreciation for Dr. Buscaglia's Passage, where he wrote, "I am beginning to believe that the truly mentally healthy individual is the one who has the most alternatives." I too have come to believe this, because I have experienced the magic of having choices.

The choice of options is for you to pick. These could be changing jobs, expanding your interest outside of work, taking regular walks, joining a nature club, or taking one more responsibility at your job to fill the time you may find to be boring with business is slow. Whatever the case, remember, alternatives are always available.

In effect, monitoring your eating patterns can help you perceive certain times when alternatives are most essential.

I know all this seems to sound so easy. But let me tell you it wasn't really. Throughout my attempts to meet wellness I very much needed to hold onto positive things and surround myself with positive people. This is not to say I did not meet with negativity, but I did try my best to circumvent it. Being in a positive environment can help you maintain positive thoughts which are vital for building confidence in yourself. If you are in the presence of encouragement and love, you are more able to love yourself and realize your worth. The worst thing a bulimic can do is remain in a situation in which she is not satisfied. You have the power to change the situation, so please, do it. It may mean risk, but these risks are necessary to lead you to live.

As I'm sure you know by now, Dr. Leo Buscaglia is someone I greatly thank for opening up my eyes to the many wonders of being myself. To conclude this chapter I want to share my favorite excerpt from his works. He writes:

"To laugh is to risk appearing the fool,
To weep is to risk appearing sentimental,
To reach out to others is to risk getting involved,
To show your feelings is to risk exposing your humanity,
To place your ideas and dreams before the crowd is to risk their loss,
To love is to risk not being loved in return,
To hope is to risk pain,
To try is to risk failure,
But risk must be taken,
Because the greatest hazard in life is to risk nothing.
The person who risks nothing does nothing has nothing and is nothing.
He may avoid the suffering and sorrow, but he simply cannot learn, feel, change, grow, live, or love.
Chained by his certitudes or addictions, he's a slave.
He has forfeited his greatest trait, and that is his individual freedom. Only the person who risks is free."

57

"*Overwhelm occurs because of an exceedingly high demand, coupled with a sense of uncertainty.*"

Sarah Boyd

OVERWHELM

One thing that I believe bulimics often suffer from is "overwhelm". From my observations, we tend to take on too much and this will trigger our binge and purge episodes. Many of us tend to have difficulty in saying no and hence our calendars become our enemy.

This can be whether we are taking too many courses, volunteering too much, balancing between business and our children, and all with this trying to maintain a healthy weight and a healthy schedule of activities.

The bulimic episodes can, in certain circumstances, be an escape for us which would be what other people would likely instead find time to meditate rather than to binge.

It is crucial that someone who has bulimia not overextends themselves so that those triggers do not come into place it may be as much as looking over a weekly schedule and realizing that there are some things that you may just have to either quit doing or reduce the time allotted for those activities to be able to make more room for the things that you enjoy doing without overstressing yourself.

OK, so this is where it all comes down to. There are so many things that made my life so painful. One of them was my father. I put him on such a high pedestal until I found out that there was something not so beautiful about him. My Disney World thinking was severely compromised.

When I found someone and I left home, I thought I could find a place that was comfortable and safe with the man I loved so much.

He was "that guy" that at 18 years old I fell in love with. I even told my best friend that I would marry him someday. Seven years later (although we did have a 3-year break due to distance), I did.

One month after our marriage I found out that he was not the man I had thought he was. He too had a secret.

I understand that it was not something that someone is proud to share, but the truth is I admitted to my bulimia before he even asked me to marry him and said I would understand if he wanted to walk away (as my last boyfriend did). He said he was okay with it. So I felt gipped that he could not be honest with me too before marriage.

When I found about his secret, my bulimia returned after having done quite well for a few months.

I did stay with him and did a lot of research. I tried to get him to open up and share his feelings, but that was impossible, other than maybe a moment or two.

Every day I wondered if his secret was important than me. "I am not good enough for him, I am not enough", I kept thinking. Our intimate life was not regular, so that did not help in those thoughts.

So I ate to fill the void of not being good enough, and not smart enough.

He was an extremely talented and very brilliant-minded person moving towards a successful life, so I kept thinking I could not get fat because that would not be a good thing. It would add to my "not enough" and I may lose him.

So, I ate my anger of thinking I wasn't good enough and I threw it up.

A year after our marriage, even knowing what I found out, I was still messed up about this man not loving me for everything that I am. I had my own business but foolishly followed him to the US from Canada, where he was starting a company. I asked if mine could cross over the border. He assured me he had spoken to his lawyers and that it would not be a problem. Once in the US, I found out that was just all a lie. More anger. I was away from my family, losing my business, and did try everything to keep it alive, not short of writing to the Senator of our State and the President of the United States. I still have the letters returned with regrets that it was not plausible. Anger. I did not want to argue the point (besides which he was quite intimidating), so I ate my anger. I sometimes wished that I had been strong enough to not hurt myself and instead speak out! But it was easier to hurt me and hide behind my anger, frustration, and disappointment by just eating and throwing it all up.

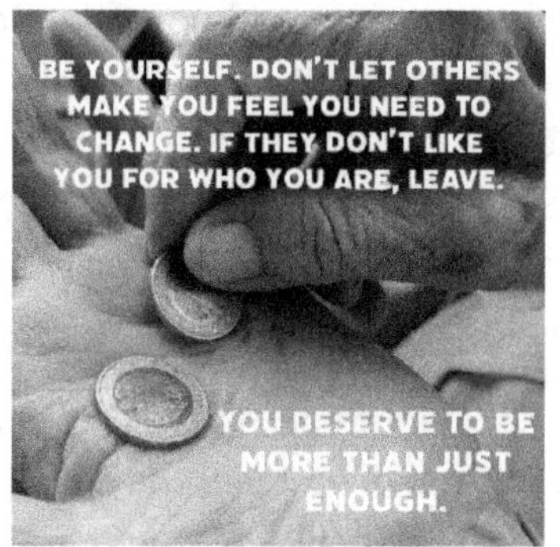

I didn't know where I fit in this world. I think that my bulimia became where I existed in this world.

I got pregnant a year and three months after our marriage (one of those precious moments in the first year I met him when his crew was there staying over). I was told I could not have children and when I told my ex-husband that I was pregnant and I was freaked out because I was still too young to have children, (no career yet and because I was too young in my mind like you would think of, Chandler on friends, "how do I do this?") he replied that it was my body and I had the choice and if I didn't want to have the child, if I did not feel ready, then that was an option.

Painful, painful, painful. How do you not have a husband who would support you to say, "I am so excited because I always wanted children" and you were told that you could not have them, and then yet he had told me the only reason to get married was to have children and when I finally got pregnant he offered me the opportunity to abort it!

I stopped throwing up and I made sure that I was going to have a very healthy child and I told him no matter what, we are having this child.

I got through the pregnancy with a beautiful boy and he was just absolutely wonderful. Oh, my goodness. Big Blue eyes. Toe Head (I found out that means white blond).

And now we have a child. And I am 20 pounds heavier.

Do you want to hear about overwhelm? My husband didn't want to take care of him at the beginning. I asked him when he was going to change diapers. He said, "it's not in the stars yet." When I was seriously in pain with what they thought was Lupus and high fever, when I asked him to feed our boy, he brought him up into the spare room where I was and handed him to me. He thought I was pretending to be in pain. Unbelievable.

I went back to work the next day after having my son, by the way. When we moved to the US and I was not able to keep my own business going, he pointed at me and said, "You are going to work for me". So, I did, and I took our son to the office. The next day he handed me a cheque to deposit at the bank. To him having a child was nothing. Ever had them cut you??? Yes, it feels like your insides are coming out if you stand too long. I didn't complain at the time. I just did it.

Overwhelm. After working in the office from the day after my son was born, I ended up working from home when he was about six months, at which time my bulimia reared its ugly head again.

Realizing it had returned, I asked my husband if I could go for counseling regarding my bulimia. Between having a child and all his friends living with us for six months while we had our child, I was just a mess. Feeding and cleaning after not just our son and him, but his crew too. He refused. I asked him to come with me as well and help me get over my bulimia and he refused.

Overwhelm.

I started to make clothes and hang out with the wife of one of his crew, who became like a sister to me. We went out dancing after the children were in bed so that my ex would not have to worry. We enjoyed ourselves, started working out at a gym, but bulimia was still present.

After too much of no contact as a couple, I wanted to go back home near my parents, sisters, and friends. We moved back to Canada. Not without hearing that it was ALL MY FAULT.

Life goes on. Four years later I want another child. I am not very fertile, but I did what I did when I got pregnant with my first one and drank some very good herbal teas and took special herbs. Within six months I did get pregnant with a beautiful daughter.

The other thing that I found out about my ex-husband is that he could not be anywhere with me without his best. This best buddy was also over at our place every time my ex-husband wasn't there. It's no wonder I love living alone today.

My bulimia seemed to have resolved itself once I was pregnant with my daughter and for two years after. My ex and I decided that maybe we should stop with our two instead of having three, as we had first agreed to. However, by the time we made that decision, I was pregnant.

The third child comes along. I enjoyed having my children. And by my third, I had already been two years free of bulimia. I loved the feeling of being a woman and feeling the baby inside of me. It was like receiving the love that my ex-husband never felt for me through his babies. I sometimes feel that I would have overcome bulimia sooner if I would have been with a man that understood that he loves me being pregnant and loves me being with child. But in the end, it appeared this man was thinking of me as his birth vessel. He even said he thought pregnant women were ugly and refused to touch my belly to feel the kick. He had no interest.

Handling three children once again brought back my overwhelm. I resumed having bulimia. I was searching for an excuse to find time alone and to myself. At times, once the children were in bed (by this time it was only at night I had bulimia attacks), I would proceed to eat my disappointment and overwhelm, then release it.

The hustle and bustle of three children, a full-time job, and trying to prove to my ex and the world that I was capable of doing everything, was too much. I even started drinking. It was like I felt that a nice body without a nice brain or a nice brain without a nice body would never be enough for my ex. I kept trying to prove myself to him trying to get his approval and trying to become his friend. Between 33 and 40 it was like a blur of volunteering, lunches, babysitters, full-time job that was very stressful.

Overwhelm.

Overwhelm continues with women into their 40s who have had to endure rough times and who wished that they could have gotten rid of their bulimia sooner, but it wasn't happening. Why? Because there was someone you allowed to be in control of your mindset. Or at least you believed that. And you couldn't find the support and love that is needed for recovery.

This exacerbated my bulimia. Again, I felt that there was nothing I could do that could be good enough for him.

At one point we decided to go to marriage counseling. The psychiatrist was wonderful. However, at one point he asked what our priorities were. Mine were husband, children, friends, then money. My husband's priorities were money first, then children, then friends, then me. OUCH.

Needless to say, our marriage ended in divorce (for other circumstances that I chose not to share here). The process of which lasted four years. It was devastating, intimidating, horrifying.

Once the final papers were signed, I ended up buying a company two hours away. My daughter, who had chosen to move in with me when I left, decided at 13 to leave me and move in with my ex and her brothers. What is the most valuable thing can a man take from you? Your children.

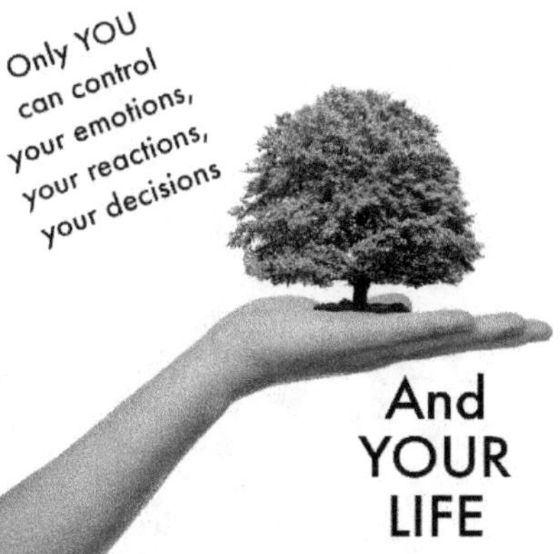

Fast forward. I was happy to be on a farm with my business and home, but I was still suffering the pain of loss. I not only now was bulimic but an alcoholic too. Nothing seemed to be enough to numb the pain and emptiness. I did meet a man a year before moving, and he was going to come with me, but I told him "no" just before I left. It was not enough. I WAS NOT ENOUGH.

For a time while I was living away, my parents told me about my niece being a drug user and how they had taken her for help, and that she was living with them. My mother was so proud of being there for her during her time of need. I thought in my mind "really Mom? And when I needed you when I was living at home and struggling with my bulimia, you just didn't want anything to do with learning more about it?" It wasn't jealousy or envy; it was DISAPPOINTMENT and another feeling that I was not good enough.

I thought moving away and having my own business would heal me. It's not so. You can't run from it. It comes with you wherever you go unless you learn the reasons and fix them inside.

I ended up losing my business, my home, almost everything material and financial. The recession combined with some wrong business decision caused me to close it down. I moved back to live with my sister for a while. The closure of the business was like another loss. Another "death" of some form.

It was during the time I was with my sister that I stopped my bulimia. I moved out, and I remained on the course towards recovery. However, I ended up with severe anxiety. I didn't want to leave my apartment. I didn't want to see anyone. I was obviously having difficulties dealing with my emotions without bulimia.

When did I end my bulimia? After the overwhelm of life? Somewhat. The truth is it was when I opened my eyes.

When I realized that I was the one in control of my life and when I stopped trying to make everybody else happy.

Why is it that simple? Well, it isn't. Absolutely not. So, I won't make you think it was. I went down and up and down and up and I'm still on a little bit of the down sometimes and a little bit of an up-down-up-down, but I look at the LaurieAnn I am today after releasing my bulimia, and it was like **releasing** that man that I felt I had to prove myself to along with everyone else, including my parents. It was no longer "having to prove" myself to others. **It was about taking care of ME!** I let go of the fact that you do not have to be perfect, but you do have to love yourself and if you don't love yourself you can't fully love anyone else, and complete recovery is almost impossible. ***(Note: You don't have to leave a relationship – as I didn't lose mine with my parents, but you do have to release the HOLD)***

Beware though. Make the right choices. Never ever falter on reviewing your choices. Don't jump in. Think things through.

And if you have children who find out about your bulimia and turn away from you and make you feel that you are/were not so perfectly perfect of a mother, don't let that worry you. In time they will work it out themselves. No mother is perfect, and children will try to find something to blame on us. It's just a fact of life. The key is YOU HAVE TO BE FIRST to be able to recover. It is not selfish in any way. It is imperative.

Interestingly enough, one of the best persons ever in my entire life was my daughter because I was honest about my bulimia with her. One day she asked if she could do a project at school about bulimia and if she could talk to me about it and at that time I was not even recovered yet, which she knew. I said absolutely. She was in grade 7. It was the best ever request I got because my daughter cared. Up to that point no one ever asked me about how I felt about being a bulimic and how it was to try and fight this, I dubbed, "stupid animal inside of me".

She asked "Mom. How does it feel?" It felt like ****. It felt like **** and I can't believe that it took my daughter to ask me that. My first family member to truly ask the questions.

The next family member was my second eldest sister who didn't ask me the questions but said that I was okay, and she knew I was still struggling. At this time, I was 48 years old. She just quietly said she worried about my health and loved me.

It was that night I realized I didn't have anyone to blame but myself for trying to please others. I had to start pleasing myself.

Recently my youngest sister said that my issues were that I would rather hurt myself than others. Self-sabotage. Bang on.

If you are overwhelmed, don't think that meditation, yoga, pills, or journaling will help alone. YOU need to make that decision that even if you look in the mirror and you see fat – that you are not seeing fat. You are seeing the part of you that your mind hasn't settled yet. And a big part of settling that is becoming friends with food. Not

fearing it. And becoming friends with your emotions. Not fearing them. And most of all, overcoming the overwhelm through not taking on too much, and when it does become too much – reach out. To a friend, a person out there willing to help, online, or on the phone. REACH OUT.

Life between your thirties and forties is quite often overwhelming and continues into the fifties for some. It's not a crime that you didn't recover after your adolescence as most people would expect. It's understandable.

A quick overview of what kind of "overwhelm" can occur during different stages of your life:

The thirties

- Young children
- Career
- Children's education
- Mortgage/Rent
- Grocery shopping

- Maintaining the household
- Trying to balance everything
- Relationship

The forties

- Teenage children
- Education
- Relationship
- Career
- Worries about the future
- Changes in the body (adult adolescence)
- Menopause
- Maintaining the household
- Trying to keep everything in balance

The fifties

- Adult children (empty nester syndrome)
- Relationship
- Sign of aging body
- Menopause
- Career
- Retirement
- For some, life changes and reinventing self

If you can add to this, please do. Be aware that these life issues can create overwhelm, the stress. If divorce is part of the factor, this can create an even greater overwhelm, such as thoughts of self-sustainability. Recovering as an adult can be a very big challenge.

If you do need to reach out, join my Facebook group www.facebook.com/groups/bullimiaddict. Know that you are NOT alone. We will go through steps of overcoming the fear of food, or of feeling alone, of being alone, of overwhelm.

"Time and health are two precious assets that we don't recognize and appreciate until they have been depleted."

Denis Waitley

FOOD, WEIGHT, AND NUTRITION

Bulimia is a vicious circle. A circle consisting of needing proper nutrition to promote better personal satisfaction with self-image, yet without the satisfaction with the self-image, it is hard to achieve proper eating behaviors. So, the question is, which is best to start with, eating well, or taking care of the emotions. Neither one is easy. The more effective one to start working with however is eating behaviors. Once you begin this, the emotions will slowly take care of themselves, with some guidance from you of course.

Having said that, let's take a quick look at the attitudes we have towards food during bulimia.

I want you to understand that I too was influenced by poor perceptions of the truth about food. It began back in the days of dieting when the amount of food consumed was not supposed to exceed the allotted caloric limitations in the regime chosen to follow. It appeared that the magic number when I started was 800 calories. Why this amount, I'm not sure. Magazine articles were everywhere, with menus of three to six tiny meals a day which added up to this number. It was often claimed that this amount was safe. The unfortunate thing is that we did not understand that a diet made up of such small quantities of nutrients is dangerous. You cannot consume a sufficient allowance of nutrients and this adds to the dangers of malnutrition. Nevertheless, without this knowledge, I continued to try following these unrealistic diets which left me frustrated each time the bingeing monster took over me.

In following these diets and eventually allowing them to become obsessions, we become overcautious of going over the daily allowances imposed on us by ourselves. It reaches the point where if we have had 813 calories, we feel that the diet has been blown and weight gain will follow. This obsessive attitude then feeds into our self-defeatist attitude. The caloric limit becomes a measurement of standards of success or failure, with no leeway for possible error. We are entrenched in the belief that even as little as 13 calories means failure and ultimately the forfeit of the possible 5 pounds we were hoping to lose in that week.

This measurement of food by calories rather than by nutritional content is what makes us lose sight of the true value of food. Calories become a means by which willpower is judged, a scale of failures and successes, a misleading guide to losing weight. We trap ourselves in such a way that our impatience and desire to lose weight quickly establish is unnatural eating behaviors in our daily routine which are unhealthy for our body and mind. Our conscious self destroys the natural balance of our subconscious self responsible for ruling the part of the mind and body which are vital for the functions of human beings. The mind, falling short of the ability to

be rational then upholds the belief that if a marginal failure of keeping within the caloric limit is present, it is best to make it turn into a big failure. Hence the binge. This, in effect, is extremism caused by self-perceived defeat.

Bulimia is used to conceal this self-defeating attitude. We hate to think that food may betray our inability to control maintaining a "perfect body size" and what is this "perfect body size"? It is unnatural thinness that is not inherent in most women or men. It is a figure which, once achieved, puts the pituitary gland into overdrive trying to balance its natural state against the forces of society's unnatural demands. Since this gland is responsible for many departments, the strain we put on several of these causes the pituitary to fail in maintaining the set balance. While it might succeed in keeping your kidneys functioning, it may fail in providing for the potential levels of adrenaline in your system or stop working on the fertility process to allow for more of its decreasing energy to stimulate the more important function of the thyroid gland.

What do we care about the extra strain the poor pituitary is working under? We want to be thin, no matter the consequences. Health becomes a secondary concern. We are too busy learning the Calories of each food. Many of us become walking calorie counters and acquire the ability to name off the number of calories in every conceivable product. We are too involved with planning the times of our binges, with trying to escape interruptions to be able to sit before the television and fill ourselves with delightful and satisfying quantities of cookies and ice cream to the point of total saturation to worry about health. In effect, we are too involved with emotional attachments to food. Food, our only friend.

I would love to know how many of us really enjoy the binges. I mean, really taste what we put into our mouths. Perhaps at the beginning, this enjoyment was present, but after a while, for me anyway, food just became a filler. Often, I wasn't even aware of what it was I wanted to fill anymore. But I didn't care. I became so secure in this little world I built. who needs anything else when food has become the comforter of pain, sorrow, and depression?

Bingo. If this is true for you too, you can be sure that you are now in the emotional whirlwind, surrounded by visions of chocolate bars and potato chips. Of empty calories. Thoughts of what could be found that are affordable and come in large quantities take over your mind. Excessive pondering over what foods will satisfy your cravings and fill your void plays on your concentration. Now it's time to stop for a while. Start trying to see food for what it is. Now you see, but you still don't want to let it go. You don't want to lose the security it has falsely blessed you with for so long. But you must at least decide to try to let it go. Some of us who have already tried this have found that the first thing we do when we try to stop abusing food is to return to those meager diets that started the whole mess in the first place. "I'll stop", you say, "as long as I don't exceed 800 calories ". Sure, go ahead. The only thing this can do for you is to lower you into further depths of

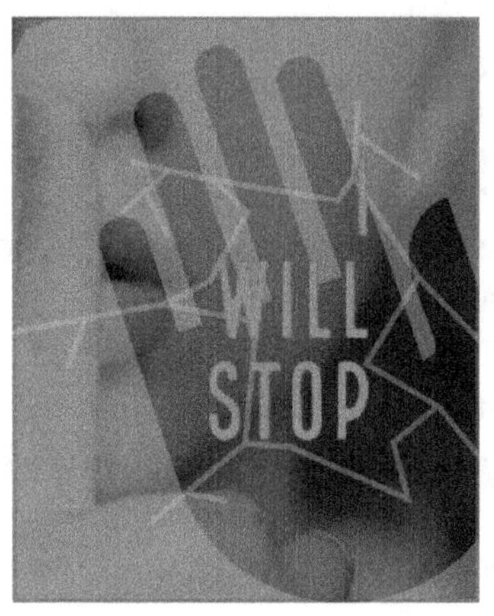

depression because the caloric limit is unrealistic and abnormal for proper physical needs. Your body will only retaliate. It will realize that during your bingeing and purging it was more likely to get more to live on because even the purging does not free you of all the food. What remains within can easily exceed these 800 calories. And while there is this excess within from the binge, the body can steal some of the nutrients before you dispose of the consumed nourishment by way of purging through self-induced vomiting, or by taking laxatives or diuretics.

The body is well equipped in case of emergencies. The signal of malnutrition is one of these emergencies. What the body does is slow its metabolism down so it can live for longer periods on what little nourishment it has been provided. It becomes quite good at this and eventually her attempts to maintain or lose weight become increasingly difficult. You panic. All of a sudden, your methods aren't working properly. So, you increase the purging frequency and the possibility of physical damage. You can't stop. Your body and your might have trapped you in a vicious circle. It's the price you are paying for being bulimic, for having voluntarily acquired a "behavior" that is of no health value. You can bet that this circle is not going to be easy to get out of, but not impossible either. The secret is to take control of the situation and realize that by continuing with the behavior, so will the struggle.

You have a choice. You can drown in despair feeling that you are too far gone and that there is no escape, or you can start filling your mind and body with the nourishment it needs to let you go. When the body and mind realize that the threat is no longer there, they will begin to let go of the chains that you feel bounded by.

During my struggle with bulimia, I knew the impact that food had on my mind, constantly lingering. I can remember the fear of being near food because of my lack of control over how much I consumed.

I can remember telling myself after each binge that it would be my last, then being terrified when someone would sit in front of me with a bag of potato chips and offer some to me. At first, I refused the offer, but my mind went through wild debates on whether to binge just one more time. The sound of chips crunching would ring through my ears like thundering beckoning calls. It was as if it wasn't translating. Luring me to have one. Have some. Have many. "You don't have to worry ", the thoughts would say, "you can always get rid of it before it takes effect on your weight ". The taste that was craved only lasted a moment before all olfactory senses were lost in the devouring of the multitude of empty caloric crisps. The person who had made the offer would look at me with awe. From a denial of wanting any to consuming nearly the entire quantity in the bag left them confused. Not to mention the fact that I could eat all that and not show any weight gain whatsoever. The question "how could you eat so much and still stay slim" became familiar. And so, did the excuses that followed. The question always produced partial guilt and partial satisfaction. I did always feel that a response was required to justify the facts. 1000 excuses were nestled in my brain, each one as convincing as the other for those who did not know about the history of my disorder. To those who had learned the secret, excuses seemed useless. They simply caused doubt to show in the face of the questioning person. In these cases, eye contact was nonexistent for fear that my eyes might speak the truth.

My school years had often restricted by bingeing to night times where my enemy, not perceived as such at the time, would rest at reach - an abundance of tempting delights.

With the end of school, however, came the end of my restriction on eating. Once I was out in the workforce, I found more time and money to support my habit. Before I knew it, I was planning binges around working hours. Food would be carefully hidden in my drawer, where my hand would slip during the slow periods. Somehow, I even managed to get around to purging within my designated hour. Before I knew it, my purging frequency was up to 8 times a day. With this increase came feelings of being forever tired and my complexion became so drawn and void of color and life, that years seem to have been added to my once youthful look.

It was after several bouts of near-fainting spells, a blurred vision, of cold sweats, of having the shakes, that I realized I wanted out of this circle. But I found it too much of an effort to get out of my lonely apartment, where I had peaceful quiet surroundings during my lonely binges. I had No Fear of being discovered in this little settlement. And this false security refused me the desire to ponder over getting involved in anything that would interrupt my hellish nightmare. It was a matter of leaving food for something else or holding onto its security. It was true. Everything had ceased to matter except the eating. The eating and purging that drew life from me, that isolated me from others, that broke up a relationship, that closed me inside myself, locked the compartment, and stashed away the key. My world.

Even through all this, I still managed to get by at work. I tried to smile and laugh to conceal the pain. At times it was difficult and my displeasure with the life I was chained to created spurts of anger which were projected through eruptions over petty problems at work. I was managing a store at the time and my workers no longer knew what to expect from me.

One day a concerned friend approached me. He had been unaware of my condition but could see the sorrow that existed behind the smile. After a lengthy conversation, I confided in him that I was suffering from depression and did not know how to get out of it. Later that day he came to visit me once again and handed me a book written by Dr. Leo Buscaglia. He assured me that by reading this book, I may find a way to face the depression. I was quite skeptical about it at first but knew that nothing could be lost. The result was a pleasant surprise. I found the book to be breathtaking as it introduced me to the concept that anything I wanted to do, I could do, and that life had things to offer that I had never even taken the time to consider, as obvious as they were. I had just been too wound-up in my own little world of negative thoughts to be bothered.

The new assurance of the other side of life was not an instant cure though. It was, however, something to work for. I cried over my

"addiction", and then that by not letting it go I would be forfeiting all the wonders I had the potential to attain. I knew that if I didn't let go of my bulimia, if I didn't unlearn it, life would pass me by. There I was, in all my self-pity, realizing for the first time that this was the greatest punishment for being bulimic. From where I sat at the bottom of my dark well, the daylight above appears to be miles away. My venture to climb to the top seemed endless. It was this venture of forgetting what was and attaining what could be that I was responsible for. I was the only one who can choose to make that climb that would define my life. I alone could break myself free of the chains food had linked me to through my own consent, locking me into a world of depression. All I needed to do was to want to get out bad enough.

In looking over my life over the years that bulimia had been present, I knew that time had come where I wanted it all to end. I wanted, deep inside, to let go of all the umbilical ties food had taken on in my mind. I wanted to let go of the deceitful friend that had imprisoned me inside myself. I wanted to let go of the fear it created. I wanted to live again.

So, the first question I asked myself was where I would begin. I chose to begin by going to a psychiatrist. My second step was to then see a doctor for an examination to know whether there was anything I would have to focus on with respect to any damages I may have inflicted on my body. After the examination, the doctor assured me that I had been lucky and that everything seemed to be functioning properly. I felt as though my ticket to ongoing life had been miraculously approved. This was also an encouragement to assure that I stay this way. The doctor, and knowledge of my condition, scheduled another appointment for six months down the road, aware of the fact that I would probably not cease bingeing and purging within a day. He was utterly understanding and quite impressed I had taken this step of admitting to my problem and wanting to do something about it.

My step was to change my attitude towards food. I needed to stop associating it with emotions and remove the fear that it was a threat. With effort, I slowly began to allow food to remain inside more frequently. To ease this process, I began with setting up a schedule of times I should eat at. This guideline helped me to keep better track of my eating behavior. In increasing the amount of food allowed to complete the journey through the digestive tract, I noticed a significant improvement in my emotional and physical state.

Stress, which was caused by lack of nourishment, caused side effects such as lower back pains and spasms in my muscles. These side effects slowly subsided with the progression towards better eating. This health improvement also helped in accepting food as its positive input outside the realm of emotional connections. As such, I knew that my time had come to break these associations with emotions once and for all. Food was the fuel that helped the body function properly, not a filler of emotional voids.

I learned to understand the nature of food. This did not automatically release me from the fear of gaining weight, but it appeased it. To further my understanding of food, I looked back to the days before dieting. Back then, I weighed 135 pounds and ate at regular intervals. This weight, having been stable for quite some time, reassured me that it was most likely the "ideal weight" for me. Consequently, once I started to let go of bulimia and began to eat properly, I allowed my weight to reach this number, all the while convincing myself that it was the right weight to be and that this weight at which I looked my best. This wasn't easy either. Having tried so hard to remain below this by 10 to 15 pounds because it was what I believe

society felt I looked best at made it difficult at times to realize that 135 was the weight at which I felt best. But once I reached this weight, I found out how wonderful it was. Because I felt healthier, my image improved, and I didn't feel fat as I thought I might have. I felt great. I was also able to eat a good amount of food which satisfied me. This reassurance helped me step off the seesaw of the scale going up and down, up, and down. My weight may not be what the crazy weight charts wanted it to be, but my weight was mine at last, not society's.

Surprisingly enough, society did not retaliate. Quite the opposite. I discovered that people around me found my true weight point to be much more appealing. I was told that I finally possessed a glow of health and that my positive emotional attitude enhanced the perspective others had of me. This positive response towards my true self became engraved in my mind and slowly wiped away the once false belief that I needed to be skinny to be accepted, liked, and perceived as success successful human being.

Everyone has a unique weight point. To find yours, you must become aware of your senses and the signals of your body. When you reach your weight point, your body functions are working at their best. Your reproductive system works on schedule, your kidneys regain the ability to regulate body fluids, sodium, and potassium concentrate, your immune systems protect you better from harmful viruses and helps in healing physical ailments caused by stress. Your weight point is your ticket to better health both mentally and physically.

To attain this weight more healthily, you must learn the value of food, food in its nourishing form. Once the nutrients foods possess are understood, you can furnish the coal your body requires to eventually develop a proper metabolic rate which will allow for proper digestion of the food you consume in proper quantity.

In the pages that follow, have included charts of vitamins and minerals to aid you in understanding the natural process they follow in your body system. In reviewing these, try to maintain the information in your memory to use it as a guide towards proper eating, while slowly letting go of the calorie guides. Calories equate food to numbers related to their energy input rather than the nutrients they provide. It is a boundary of numerals setting the standard of measurement not significant enough to gain knowledge of the true value of food.

One young lady who had had bulimia one time said that she objected to pamphlets that stated that a young woman needs to consume 2000 calories a day on average. She claimed that it was misleading to believe that 2000 calories would not allow for weight gain. After years of following the calorie counting method as a guide to how much to eat, this misconception is quite understandable. The fact is, however, that it is possible to consume this amount without weight gain. It is all relative. It is relative to the amount of activity one is involved in, relative to the sort of activity one does, relative to the size and weight of the person, relative to the kind of calories that are being consumed. If the calories are comprised primarily of proper quantities of food from the four food groups (dairy, bread, and cereals, fruit and vegetables and meat, fish, and poultry), with one 10th allowed for "empty calories ", The odds of weight stability are greater, even if the amount reaches 2000 calories.

If you learn to categorize food by its nutritional value rather than caloric, you can create a proper attitude towards the consumption of these nutrients, and eventually, you can become comfortable with your eating behavior in realizing that quality, not numerical quantity, is the key to better eating. As well, by following the little signal that tells you when you require food, or when you have had enough, you can learn to understand the needs of your body concerning the number of nutrients it requires to function best.

So, let go of those calories. It may be a slow process to be able to do this, but even while you are still holding on to this way of categorizing food, try to remember that it is a method lacking proper projection of what foods are worth.

In learning about the nutritional value of food, you should not start denying yourself groupings of food that are low in nutrients. You must continue to allow to have these and learn to implement them into your eating pattern. Often it is this group that is based on a craving. Tell yourself that you can have these in reasonable quantities without indulging in them to an excessive degree, and you will. Learn to understand that a desirable quantity of such foods

will not add those pounds you fear and in doing so you will be in a better position to achieve your goal of removing the threat you believe them to have.

Another consideration to keep in mind would be to stop stepping on the scale every day, as many of us tend to do. This is deceiving. Your own body knows the weight you should be at. No man-made object can direct you the way your body can. To follow the numbers on a scale as a guide to what weight you should be at will only serve to obstruct your ability to see yourself as you are, and that is usually a person desiring to be at a healthy weight - yours. The other thing is that when you step on the scale daily, it can set off your mood. If it tips upwards, it can ruin it. You don't want to start your day that way.

The charts that follow outlined the function of the vitamins and minerals, the required daily allowance, the benefits of having sufficient quantities, and the source where they are found. I have purposely avoided writing about the symptoms that may occur from deficiencies of such vitamins and minerals, feeling that at this point it is preferable for you to stay away from negativity. The benefits alone will help you to understand the need for these. Following the charts on vitamin and mineral minerals, I have included a listing of some of the foods that are usually categorized as "empty calorie" foods. Next to these, I have included the nutrients they possess, as well as the daily percentage these foods allow for. My objective here is to help you become better acquainted with the other side of junk food - the positive side. Though the nutrient quantity is indeed low in these, is not to say that they are without any at all. When you understand this, you can develop a better attitude towards them in knowing that they are not entirely free of nutrients. Perceived as such, you can let go of the feelings that you are simply taking in food that is adding to your weight rather than helping to add to the nutritional intake of your day.

BASIC CHART FOR VITAMINS AND MINERALS

VITAMINS/MINERALS AND QUANTITY	BENEFITS	SOURCE
A	Needed for vision, skin,	Green plants, yellow veggies, fish liver oil,

700mcg/day	mucous membrane reproduction	egg yolk, milk, butter, cream, carrots
B1 1 – 1.5mg/day	Produces energy, appetite, enhances digestion and immunity	Wheat germ, cereal, pasta, nuts, beans, whole wheat, oysters, pork, liver, asparagus, apples, lemon, grapefruit, celery, cabbage, carrots, coconut
B2 1.2-1.7mg/day	Healthy skin, enhances immunity, vitality	Liver, milk, spinach, leafy vegetables, dairy products, crabmeat, broccoli, mushrooms, oyster, whole wheat, beans, apples, carrots, coconut, grapefruit
B6 2-2.2mg/day	Increases immunity	Liver, avocados, green beans, bananas, whole wheat
B12 3-4mcg/day	Decreases stress, which means increased immunity	Liver, kidney, eggs, milk, oysters, meat, fish
Folic Acid 800mcg/day	Helps the healing process	Spinach, liver, kidney, wheat germ
C	Quick healing, prevents fatigue	Apples, oranges, pineapple, beans, broccoli, parsley, green peppers, cucumber, spinach, grapefruit, tomato, cabbage, asparagus,

		carrot, strawberries, banana, potatoes
B3 12-20mg/day	Enhances immunity system	Liver, poultry, meat, tuna, grains, nuts, beans, peas
D 400IU/day	Nerve relaxer, energy booster, forms tooth and bone	Cod liver, egg yolks, milk, sunshine, fish
E 30IU/day	Good for reproduction system, glandular system, and muscle function	Oils from vegetables, cod liver oil, oatmeal, rye, yellow cornmeal, whole wheat, butter, brown rice, eggs, cheese, fish, beans, Brussel sprouts, parsley, spinach, carrots, celery, lettuce, popcorn, cabbage, apples, bananas, liver, kidneys, nuts
Calcium 800-1500mg/day	Reduces stress, prevents blood clotting, strengthens teeth and bones	Milk, leafy greens, broccoli, spinach, carrots, celery, grapefruit, sardines, lemon, orange, parsley, almonds, cheese
Chloride 9mg per kg/day	Keeps hair and mind healthy	Raw meat, salt, milk, legumes, tomato, olives
Copper 6mg/day	Prevents anemia, increases energy	Molasses, liver, clams, egg yolks, dried fruit, leafy greens, whole wheat

Iron 18mg/day	Help to give rosy complexion, vitality and enhances immunity	Uncooked leafy greens, liver, kidney, wheat germ, peanuts, fruits, egg yolk, parsley, clams, spinach, dates, whole wheat, beans, cabbage, tomato
Magnesium 400mg/day	Help keep bones and teeth healthy, dissolves kidney and gallstones, and prevents constipation and poor circulation	Nuts, milk, egg yolk, whole wheat, legumes, brown rice, spinach, orange, dates, raisins
Phosphorous 1000mg/day	Keeps hair, nails, and skin healthy, bones and teeth strong	Meats, milk, eggs, cheese, peas, nuts, beans, wheat
Potassium 2000-2500mg/day	Helps heart muscle to function properly, helps relaxation, and proper kidney function	Bananas, cantaloupe, wheat germ, green vegetables, raisins, dried fruit, potatoes, nuts, olives, milk
Zinc 15mg/day	Speeds healing	Red meat, milk, liver, seafood, eggs, whole wheat
Sodium	Helps to better heart function, decreases heartburn, and strengthens bones	Muscle meats, most veggies, sea and table salt, whole wheat, cheese, bananas
Sulfur	Keeps hair, skin,	Milk, cheese, eggs,

	and nails healthy, and increases immunity	nuts, cabbage, Brussel sprouts, cereal, most fruit, most vegetables

THE JUNK FOOD LIST

PRODUCT	NUTRIENT	% OF DAILY REQUIREMENTS
Sara Lee Chocolate Cake 1/8 of a cake	Protein Vitamin A Vitamin C Iron	2 2 2 6
Cracker Jacks 1 ounce	Protein Iron	2 4
Fig Newtons 2 cookies	Protein Thiamine (B1&B2) Calcium Iron	2 2 2 4
Oreo Chocolate Sandwich Cookies 3 cookies	Protein Iron	2 4
Pillsbury Chocolate Chip Cookie Dough 2 cookies	Protein Thiamin Iron	3 6 5
Aunt Jemima Original (recently retired) 3 4: pancakes (1/4 cup milk, ½ tbsp oil, ½ egg)	Protein Vitamin C Thiamine Calcium Iron	8 2 6 2 6
Pillsbury Best Apple Danish	Protein Thiamine	4 8

One	Iron	6
Totino's Party Cheese Pizza	Vitamin A	8
	Vitamin C	4
	Thiamine	15
½ pizza	Calcium	25
	Iron	8
Fritos Corn Chips	Protein	2
	Calcium	2
15 Chips	Iron	2
Orville Redenbacher Gourmet Popcorn	Protein	4
	Iron	4
4 cups plain		
Regular Potato Chips	Protein	2
	Vitamin C	10
15 Chips	Thiamine	2
	Iron	2
Vanilla Ice Cream (basic)	Protein	6
	Vitamin A	6
½ cup	Thiamine	2
	Calcium	10

INFORMATION AND HELP

Back in the days when my bulimia first began, there was little information readily available on the disorder. I was first able to receive some literature on the subject from the United States, thanks to an article in a magazine that listed the address of a hospital where they had established a department for eating disorder research. I wrote to the address with great anticipation for the reply. When it arrived, however, a handful of studies primarily on anorexia nervosa was all the contents held. The restricted information was upsetting. To add to this frustration was the fact that bulimia had not had a great part in the studies and mention of this disorder usually held a position within the context of the research on anorexia. The disappointment for me stemmed greatly from the fact that though anorexia and bulimia had certain similar characteristics, I did not categorize them as the same disorder.

Today you do not have to go to the United States for information, and research on anorexia does not take precedence anymore. Separate studies have become available for bulimics, which can help to better comprehend the subject through a more detailed analysis.

As I go along, I will give you some idea of how to acquire such information. I will also discuss the different kinds of help available to you.

Before proceeding, I would like to take some time to advise you that though it has been said that bulimia cannot be corrected without professional help. This is not true. There have indeed been some cases where people have been able to conquer bulimia on their own. One lady who has achieved this now holds self-help workshops and shares her experience with others. Though professional help can be of great value, do not dismiss the self-recovery altogether. It may be good for some to know that this can be done, especially those who are in secluded areas where help is not readily available. As well, in today's world, with the ability to be online face to face, this has been positive for those with this disorder seeking to recover.

In my case, for the first four years, I tried to overcome bulimia alone, but it was in vain. The extended period I put into fighting this disorder without success finally led me to get support. One day I noticed an article in a local newspaper announcing that an organization composed of self-help groups for bulimics and anorexics was being formed. With the desire to see that bulimia meet its end, I called the given number and receive the address of where the next meeting was to be held.

Unfortunately, the outcome of this visit was devastating. I found myself in a state of even greater depression once the meeting was over. I'm not quite sure why it was that I was affected in this way. I would assume that it was particularly the cause of negativity in all those who were present at the meeting. Anger and depression were bountiful in the discussions. Needless to say, it was my first and last attendance.

Life continued as usual for me, until one year passed and I moved into a place of my own, having decided not to follow my parents who were being transferred East. I felt that being on my own may be the solution to easing the recovery. This was soon proved wrong. Within one month of my parents' absence, binges had increased to 8 times a day. This went on for nearly six months until I just couldn't take it anymore.

My next endeavor was to make an appointment with a psychiatrist. I found one who specialized in eating disorders and set up a time at which to meet with her. Her fees were a mere $60.00 per hour and my company had coverage for 1/3 of this amount.

On my way to the psychiatrist's office, I tried very hard to relax, but I could not control the palpitations in my heart, nor the knots in my stomach. I arrived at the location and was led into a room, where there was a couch, a desk, a scale, and a chair. I sat on the couch and waited. Minutes later I was greeted by a lady much the same height as me, but whose weight must have been half of mine. I looked at her curiously. She sat in the chair opposite me and proceeded to ask me questions. She handed me a stack of schedules I was to fill out which was to record my eating behavior, then she weighed me. Her voice was cool and monotonous, her eyes void of any emotions.

The session carried on for one hour. Near the end of our meeting, the doctor discussed health. She asked if there were any discomforts I could tell her about. At first, my mind blanked out, but I soon regained composure and remembered some of the troubles I was having. The first of these was my heart palpitations. Remaining calm, the doctor glanced at me momentarily, then told me that I would have to see a physician as soon as possible. Her unmelodious words explained that I may have been suffering from electrolyte imbalances, a condition that had accounted for Karen Carpenter's death. My heart palpitated at that instant as horror swept through my body. Was I going to die?

As I left her office, I was overcome by feelings of loneliness and fear. What I thought was going to be a visit that would motivate and encourage me to get well ended up as a nightmare which created concern and worry for my health and well-being. I went home to a restless night, afraid that if I slept, I would not awaken. The distress was so great that I could not bring myself to see the psychiatrist again for fear that I may only get another dose of panic to add to the one I already possessed.

On my own accord, I found a doctor and went to see him for an examination. I told him about my eating disorder. The doctor looked at me with puzzling eyes. "Bulimia? What exactly was bulimia?" he asked. I sat there with tears streaming down my face, trying desperately to explain it to him between sobs. When I told him that I was purging my food by way of self-induced vomiting and had increased the number to eight times a day, he stared with disbelief. But his eyes were filled with comforting compassion as he asked me if I had any knowledge of what problems might have developed from this disorder. I explained to him the best I could what the possible outcome could be, from the electrolyte imbalance to the possible kidney damages, to the increase of stress through malnutrition.

Ten days after the examination took place, I was called back in to see the doctor. He sat me down and went over the test, explaining what each one meant. Over the 10 days, he had read up on the disorder so that he could be familiarized with the areas to look for possible damages. This reassurance gave me comfort in knowing that I was being cared for properly.

The test results showed that I was still healthy and that my electrolytes were still balanced. There were signs of malnutrition, however, which were apparent from the high protein content in my urine. The doctor advised me that another examination should follow in three months. With proper eating within this time, he assured me that the signs of malnutrition should disappear. But the rest was up to me.

I was encouraged by the good results of the test but felt alone in my attempts to get well. I had tried twice to seek support but had found no comfort in either. My next choice, therefore, was to try to do it myself with more determination than ever. I had to want to get well to help myself to do it. It was about this time when I was suddenly overwhelmed with external pressures. My bulimia, which had robbed my body of many nutrients, left me susceptible to strains that stress from these external pressures produced. As such, physical problems began to surface.

My trips to the doctor's office became so frequent that I was finally advised to slow down. The doctor knew that many of the symptoms were the result of my inability to cope with stress. I was presented with a diet plan the doctor made of relaxing exercises to be done nightly. This, he advised me, would be the way I could overcome much of the physical ailments and perhaps even the emotional ones I was experiencing.

Unfortunately, words did not suffice. Every day seemed to increase the fear that I was going to die, that the physical problems were the cause of deadly diseases that were announcing that my time had come.

"NO!" Finally, I stood up and said "NO!" I was not going to let myself fall any lower. I packed up my belongings put them in my car and headed to where my parents were, 2000 miles away. I decided that I had to go to my family. I had to leave the place that was seemingly saturated with the unfortunate. I had to go and change the scenery of my life and start fresh. I needed to, and I did it.

The move was not the solution to the problem. As I moved back into my parents' home, I only found controlling my behavior to be as hard as ever. I tried extremely hard though and had managed to decrease the bingeing to one to three times daily. It was a good feeling to know that there had been an improvement, but it just wasn't enough.

Parental restrictions, which I had been without for nearly a year, had become hard to handle. They created a feeling of being trapped and were causing problems in a new relationship I was involved in. The strain they were putting on me rolled over into my attempts to get well. The top of the well was moving away from me again. Once again, I had to make a choice. This time I wanted to make a choice that would be the key to finally letting go of my bulimia. It had to be made, once and for all.

My choice was to move away from home, all the while remaining close enough to my family to be able to see them whenever their presence was needed. I needed the freedom I was used to, and the ability to spend more time on my relationship. So, I found a place to stay and a job near my home.

From that day, my luck seemed to ride alongside me. One day at work I received a phone call from a young lady who was looking for a way to advertise her services. The company I worked for at the time specialized in nutritional advertising. This lady hoped that our assistance could be of benefit to her. Unfortunately, the sum of our advertising services was above her means. In wishing to help her in finding some other solution, I inquired as to what aspect of nutrition she worked on. It so happened that she was a therapist for people with eating disorders and worked with these patients in trying to increase their understanding of the nutritional value of foods. I felt a strange feeling of relief as if by some chance, fate had made her call my number. I explained to her that

I was unable to help in advising her of an alternative, but that I could assist her in acquiring another patient if she was interested. She was.

At the time I made my first appointment, Suzanne's office, which was in her home, was being renovated. We decided, therefore, on alternative arrangements and chose the lobby of a downtown hotel as our meeting place. Descriptions of our appearance were made the best they could for easy recognition for our rendezvous. And so, two days after the call we met. From the first time I saw her, I knew that this lady was going to be the link to my recovery.

The atmosphere of being in public was comforting. It created an atmosphere much like meeting a friend for a drink after work. Suzanne sat next to me and began asking me to tell her about my history of bulimia. It seemed that I could have gone on forever, but I made sure to keep to the particulars.

Once my report was complete, Suzanne took over the conversation. She acknowledged that the steps I had taken towards my independence seemed positive and that physically I had no sign of immediate danger. At this point, she went off on a different tangent and started to focus on the positive aspects of my being.

There seemed to be a special understanding that Suzanne possessed in the value of staying away from the discussion of possible physical problems that may have been created through bulimia. Her primary concern, rather, was that of assuring me that there was nothing to worry about. When she handed me the telephone number of a doctor she recommended, 

she explained that the rest was up to me, and the discussion on the physical aspect was laid to rest.

The choice of acquiring Suzanne's help proved to be even more advantageous than I had imagined. Not only did I find the locations of our meetings appealing to my character, but she also allowed for flexibility in the frequency and times of appointments. I was grateful for this. I have always been one who is likely to stick to something which allows me the freedom to choose the times which I felt best suited for the appointments. Feeling obliged to set aside one specific day every week for something has long since been difficult for me to do. As long as I knew that she would see me whenever the need was present, I knew that I would continue to want to see her.

Within a week of our first meeting, I had set up an appointment to see the doctor. Once again, the results were positive. Two weeks after receiving the results, I met once again with Suzanne, and together we went over them. She advised me on certain eating patterns I may want to work on, that once again proceeded to discuss positive matters outside of bulimia.

For one year the meetings continued. With each one, I felt Suzanne's positive attitude built my esteem and strengthened the belief I had in myself. And with each rejuvenated feeling of self-worth, came a decrease in my bingeing.

Through the course of our sessions, Suzanne and I discussed aspects of my relationship, of my job, and of reasons why my bingeing was triggered. She helped me conclude that boredom was a great threat to my good eating, as well as fatigue and alcohol. With each realization, Suzanne would discuss with me the alternatives and help me to see things objectively and clearly. She had confidence in my recovery and did all she could to make sure that I acquired this confidence too.

Meetings were often monthly, with the occasional extra meeting in between. The one month between the meetings made for a period where I could learn to fend for myself. This pending was eased in knowing that if I ever felt that I couldn't make it through, Suzanne was just a phone call away. I began to learn to find alternatives on my own, which strengthened my character and made me realize that I could solve my problems.

Many little pointers served as great helpers in my recovery. Suzanne had taught me how to jump the barriers that often stood in the way of my recovery. I learned to stop and think things over rationally, to build my awareness of my feelings, to acknowledge what was right in my life and what wasn't, and to work on what wasn't.

What my experience shows is that there are several means by which you can get help, and two, that it is imperative to find that one that suits you best. For me, it was having a therapist who allowed for a comfortable environment outside of an office and which allowed for flexibility. For you, it may well be the self-help group, or perhaps the psychiatrist, or psychologist, or like me, the therapist, or even today the counselors, or the coaches. The self-help group is usually the more affordable alternative, followed by the therapist or the counselor or the coach, the psychologist, and finally the psychiatrist. In the case of Suzanne, she worked out her rates on a sliding scale to accommodate those who were short of money. Of course, if you feel that you have what it takes, the other alternative is to do it on your own. The choice is yours.

Now let me give you an idea of what each form of help can offer you.

The self-help group is comprised of people suffering from eating disorders, usually a combination of bulimics and anorexics. The idea behind the meetings is to allow each individual to share their feelings with the others towards their disorder and the effects it has had on their lives, their relationships, and themself. The positive aspect of group meetings is that it assures you that you are not alone in your struggles and that others are willing to share these feelings with you. On the other hand, group meetings may induce depression if the discussions deal mainly with the negative characteristics of the disorders. This was what had occurred at the self-help group I had tried to join. There had not been anyone to input positive direction into the conversation. Given this, if you do choose to go this route, make sure that the person or persons who are heading the group can make you feel that there is a way to relieve the depression. Usually, this is available when there is a reformed bulimic speaking in the group.

The second form of help you can acquire is with either a psychiatrist, a psychologist, a therapist, a counselor, or a coach. As an individual seeking support of this kind, you gain a more personalized level of help. For me, this was the most efficient support, but only once I met up with someone compatible with me. It is especially important to feel at ease with the person you are meeting with. Again, they should have the ability to create a positive environment to help build your self-esteem and your confidence that recovery is possible. it may take time to find the right person, but do not let yourself get discouraged, as I had let myself. To do so only means prolonging the disorder. If you need help to find someone, you can call your local hospital and inquire about possible reference lists they may have for doctors dealing with eating disorders or you can Google particularly if you want to be specific to bulimia. There are people who specialize in that specific category.

The third possibility for help is 1 where you are admitted into a hospital for treatment this is usually suggested only in the case when the person suffering from the disorder is in physical danger and needs immediate attention. Some places will interview the patient to assess how important it is that the person is admitted. Others, where physical problems are apparent, will not require the interview. In essence, this form of therapy does is monitor the patient more closely and try to prepare them for when they are released from the hospital.

When dealing with support from a professional, there are different therapies available. These may include focusing on helping the patient gain weight properly and encourage exercise programs to accompany this; concentrating on dealing with the attitudes and perceptions of the patient and working on reversing the false beliefs that have been acquired and are feeding the self-defeating self; analysis of the experience of a patient, focusing on earlier relationships and trying to connect the possible influence they may have had in bringing on the disorder.

Family therapy is used most often in cases where the patient is a child. Family members are counseled on how to deal with and how to help in supporting the patient through recovery.

Therapy or coaching involving educating the patient on the nutritional value of food, coupled with positive thinking, I believe, is the most effective in helping a bulimic out of the circle. That is my opinion, all the while respecting those who prefer other forms.

When and if you decide that you do want to get outside support, odds are you will feel apprehension and following the decision through. It is not an unfamiliar feeling. Believe me. The main thing is not to think yourself out of it. If you sense this is the right choice, then get to it as soon as possible before Mr. Doubt takes precedence. This is especially important if you have tried to overcome bulimia on your own but have not succeeded.

Let go of the fear of admitting that help would be to your advantage. When you can come to terms with this, you will be in the right position to know that what you are doing is the best conceivable resolution for you.

Initial help can be sought in two primary ways. The first of these is by seeing your family doctor. Never fall under the false assumption that going to your doctor and telling him that you have a disorder will mean that you will immediately be admitted into an institution. This is not so. For one, telling the physician of your condition is beneficial in that he or she can have a better idea of what to look for in the outcome of your examination. The second advantage is the possibility of acquiring a referral to a professional who deals with eating disorders through your doctor. In some areas, psychiatrists will only take patients who have been referred to them. In some instances, this is because of the law. Psychologists and therapists, counselors, and coaches, however, are more easily accessible, as such rules less likely pertain to their practice.

If seeing your doctor is not your preference, then you have the alternative of getting directly in touch with a therapist, psychologist, therapist, counselor, or coach, or even a self-help group. It is advised that a physician be consulted at some point in time, however, to be able to be attentive to possible physical ailments that may have emerged during your disorder. Usually, you will be told which vitamins and or mineral supplements would be best to take, and what deficiencies you may have. But fear not. If you are still functioning at a healthy level, your visit to the doctor will simply assure you that you have little to worry about right away.

There is one more way I would like to discuss whereby those suffering from disorders may find relief in communicating about their disorder. I will call this "correspondence therapy ".

A few years ago, I acquired an address from an organization in my city of a young lady who had been suffering from bulimia and desired to write to someone else who could share their experience. The prospect of helping another by way of Mail pleased me, as I greatly enjoyed writing and found this to be one of the better ways I expressed myself. With great anticipation, I wrote the first letter. The response I

received was from a person who was in great despair over her disorder. There was nothing positive about this first letter. I wrote back in an attempt to get her to respond to what she perceived as a positive input in her life. Once again, there was nothing she could submit to me of this nature. She asked me to listen to her, but to refrain from reaching out. She claimed that she did not need anyone and did not want anyone to try to get close to her. It was not enough to discourage me. I replied that I would not let anyone tell me to stop being compassionate, that I was going to try to reach her regardless of her request that I not, as I was not about to simply stand by and read about the fear and pain of another without at least endeavoring to breakthrough. The next letter from my friend proved what I expected. She broke down, admitting that the help would be of great value to her and that she was never so grateful for my persistence.

The contents of our letters rarely touched on the aspects of food, but rather we used to find alternatives for her behavior. I queried about possible interest she may have had, positive characteristics she believed she possessed and how these could be used to help her recover. After one year of this type of correspondence, I received the most rewarding letter of reply. She announced that her bingeing and purging had decreased from six times daily to one to two times. She had approached a close friend and told him of her secret. She assured me that he was very understanding and provided her with an immediate outlet whenever things seem to be getting tough. My pen pal assured me that this was one of the best possible steps she could have taken. This confidant was strong and stood by her all the way, supporting her through the recovery, and allowing room for error when she fell short of her desired expectations.

Another month passed before I heard from her again. The letter assured me that the silence had not been intended, but that she had become quite busy with outside interests and this left her little time for correspondence. With this increase in activity, she confirmed that she was even nearer to her goal. She had since decreased the frequency of her binges now two once a week. With each letter that announced her growing success came greater sweeps in her writing, the pages glowing with artistic swoops and curls that appeared at the end of each word. A sign of growing confidence from a young lady who had once believed that bulimia had been her only friend and that she would never want to let it go. Now she wanted out altogether and felt the victory of feeling greater health and less dependence on the addiction.

From this wonderful experience, I gained a wonderful friend. In one of the letters, she claimed that everyone should have a friend like me. But it is not a matter of everyone having a friend like me, but rather a matter of everyone having a true friend to lean on and to help you through the rough times. It was not just one-sided. She had helped me too, as I had her. She gave me encouragement to go on, encouragement to stay well and backed up the belief that love is the strongest healer of pain. I greatly admire her and always will. Our letters continued across the country for several years as we continued to share our joys and at times sorrows. It now seems that the good outweighs the bad with the improvement of the self-esteem and the benefits we gained through our alternatives. The greatest lesson learned was that even though we were faceless to each other, we found a friendship that was warm and touching. A warmth that bulimia could never provide, only another human being.

I am hoping that this form of therapy will soon be implemented into programs across the country. I, for one, am implementing it into my bulimia recovery coaching program. I will be glad to receive any postal mail from those who are either in remote areas who are too afraid to face another person at this time, be it face to face or online. With the ability to communicate via postal mail, I believe that many can take the first steps without the fear of confrontation. This also has another advantage in that it is a method by which the person suffering from bulimia can read her personal feelings on the pages before her. This person can also notice the changes in their handwriting while so doing. This will shed a clearer light on many aspects of the journey towards recovery. It's a way of releasing the tension all the while knowing that someone else out there, who has or is sharing the same feelings or is helping the person is understanding you and holding onto a piece of paper that you took the time to write your feelings and your thoughts on.

One last note for those who believe that they would like to try to recover alone. I cannot guarantee that it would be beneficial to you, but you may want to try finding someone, much like my pen pal had, to listen to you. To do this, however, you must be confident that the person with whom you are confiding is someone who has patience and understanding and who can guide you towards more positive outlets and a clear perception of your true self. I do caution that there may be a risk in this. A risk that perhaps your judgment may have been wrong and the person may react differently. But it's a risk worth taking when the outcome is a shoulder to lean on.

Reading up on the disorder often becomes obsessive for bulimics. No matter how tiny an article, our eyes become like those of a hawk and we find these with as much ease as if our name itself was printed on it. We read so much about the disorder that we come to believe that we know everything there is to know about it, that we have become experts on the subject. That's fine and may well be near the truth, but it can also create problems. When help is sought, you may assume that the person helping you knows less than you do, mainly because they have not had the personal experience of going through what you have. This may even go as far as threatening your chances of letting them help you properly. Very well, you know a lot about the disorder. But like me, you are probably not a doctor and could not, therefore, know everything there is to know about the medical aspects, and may even fail to objectively understand the psychological aspects as well. Just because you have read every book an article there is on the subject, and you have experienced it as well, don't assume that the one who is dealing with it on a professional level is not more learned than you are. These professionals learn from you, but they have also learned from many others and have often seen many more sides of the coin than you have. This is where their experience exceeds yours. Work with them, share your knowledge, and listen to theirs. It's a team effort, so play it right. Continue to read, to learn about the disorder. Most of all learn that you are not alone, that many others have suffered from the same things you are suffering from, and that there are people around to help you.

Information on disorders can be obtained from several different sources. Many more hospitals today have departments assigned specifically to deal with eating disorders. Some associations have been created to provide information by way of websites, social media groups, printed literature in pamphlets, or newsletters, and provide a good source for those with the disorder, as well as for family members, coaches, and teachers. There are books as well that deal with anorexia nervosa and bulimia, and these are listed at the back of this book in the chapter "other readings ".

Whatever the help you get, remember, it's there, so use it. Use it to create a better life. You can't imagine the wonder of being free of bulimia. It's a high no amount of food could ever supply you with because it's a high elevated from the real you, the you who can finally live.

"The main health hazard in the world today is people who don't love themselves."

Kinky Friedman

HEALTH HAZARDS – PHYSICAL AND EMOTIONAL

Perhaps one of the most difficult things for a bulimic to face up to is the emotional and physical health hazards bulimia could be responsible for. Like a smoker being confronted with the outcome of smoking - cancer - yet does not find this to be sufficient motivation to quit, so it is with the bulimic. Often, we are aware of the health hazards our behavior threatens us with, but we just often wish to ignore them. It becomes a matter of thinness versus health.

As mentioned before, emotional disruptions originate primarily from the initial dieting which leads to eating disorders. We, the bulimics, are often ignorant of the fact that proper health generally involves a harmonious balance between the satisfaction of the physical self and positive feelings towards one's character. There is seemingly even further oblivion to the fact that it is the brain that generates these attributes. Without proper fueling by the way of nutrients, the brain locks the necessary energy to function properly, and in effect, a temporary malfunction occurs, leading to emotional instability.

The purging that coexists with bingeing and bulimia, rob the body of many necessary vitamins and minerals which are crucial elements in the brain's ability to fend off negative attitudes.

Joan Borysenko, Ph.D., Author of the book Minding The Body, Mending The Mind sites that the feeling of helplessness - which is common in bulimics - upsets the balance of hormones and lowers the resistance to disorder. This, in turn, disrupts the areas of the brain that controls emotion, this area being greatly dependent on the chemicals created by the immune system. As such, chronic helplessness occurs. Chronic helplessness then depletes the chemicals required for feelings of joy and satisfaction. Eventually, the victim develops stress from this and the loss of control over stress creates even lower levels of resistance to disorder. Dr. Borysenko Writes that "we learn to be helpless, and the resultant depressed behavior then feeds on itself ".

Prolonged bulimia is indicative of uncontrolled negativity. Vomiting depletes us of potassium, vitamin B, and vitamin C which are needed in combating stress. Greater stress developed still with the negativity induced by malnutrition. And like a circle, stress then fees are depression, which feeds are stress, which fees are depression. Depression works on other parts of our thinking behavior by creating feelings of low self-esteem. So as long as the brain isn't recompensed for its lost nutrients, the reversal of depression becomes toilsome, if not impossible.

Other vitamin and mineral deficiencies from semi-starvation, coupled with the effects of stress, trigger yet other weaknesses. Insufficient protein, vitamin E, and or vitamin A comma as well as others, threaten the process of healing. The brain cannot delegate the shortage of nutrients to the necessary parts of the anatomy to do a proper job, and as such, physical problems occur.

Physical problems arising from prolonged bulimia can be anything from dehydration, to gastroenteritis, to constipation and diarrhea, to fainting spells, to periods of cold sweat and blurred vision, to lower back pains, to headaches, to irregular menstrual cycles, to water retention, to electrolyte imbalance, to kidney dysfunction or discomfort. In extreme cases, death.

Bulimia has also been known to cause corrosion of the tooth enamel from stomach acid, excessive cavities, and even temporomandibular joint dysfunction, which is the dislocation of the jaw.

Again, like a circle, these physical ailments put pressure on the emotional state. The development of low immunity to both physical and emotional stresses may even lead bulimics to an eventual breakdown. This is what occurred to me. In the fifth year of my bulimia, I became more aware of the physical problems I was having. At the same time, this arose, I also had many external pressures to face. I tried to concentrate solely on external problems, but my efforts were in vain. Everything around me and within me seemed to be falling apart. Before I knew it, I was seeing the doctor every week with an inflamed lower back one day, excruciating pains in the right side of my head the other, strep throat the other, and finally pains in my neck. I was becoming just that - a pain in the neck. But the doctor remained patient and tried his best to diagnose each one to my satisfaction. He assured me that I was not dying. My lower back pains were caused by muscle spasms coupled with a minor infection in the lower part of my pelvic region. My strep throat was due to my low resistance to disorder and the pain in my neck was most probably caused by tension. All of these were caused by stress. The only thing this doctor could not diagnose was the pain in my head. I continued to pursue this, and five months later, and five doctors later, it was found to be the dislocation of the jaw (TMJ). With all the internal and external turmoil, I finally was ripped apart until I couldn't handle it anymore. Thus, the "nervous breakdown". It was just during this time that I received my first book by Dr. Leo Buscaglia, and it was then I made my decision to get well. But it would be a while before the conquest.

In the end, I felt grateful that the damages I had allowed my body to undergo were not life-threatening.

When you decide to visit your physician, take my advice - tell him or her about the bulimia. It is the only way he or she will be able to best help in looking for the vital areas of possible damage. Pamphlets on balanced diets may also be acquired from these visits. It is well worth the truth.

I would like to note here that during your recovery, you will likely continue to binge occasionally. In this case, I would greatly advise that substantial amounts of water be consumed. Bulimics are very susceptible to dehydration, and this dehydration can create problems with the function of your liver, kidneys, and bladder. After you purge, try to drink water to re-establish the level of fluid in your body requires.

I realize that this may be difficult to get used to, as the habitual step on the scale to record the success of your endeavors to free yourself from the food you ate may be thrown off with the excess fluid. But you can make yourself understand that the weight that is gained from water is just that – water. By drinking the proper amount, you can help your body avoid at least part of the struggle you have created for it. Believe me, I know. I have had to face the dread of dehydration, and it is not something I wish on even my greatest enemies. So, take my word. Drink. But one word of caution. Try to stay away from alcohol and colas (even diet). These only add to the problem of dehydration. So, if you follow my advice, try to keep either water or if you are comfortable enough, try juices. But do drink!

"Sometimes, after a storm, people say there was no warning. There was a warning, but nobody was listening."

Jeff Last

WARNING SIGNALS FOR PARENTS, SPOUSES, PARTNERS & RELATIVES

Any bulimic reading this chapter will unequivocally condemn me for revealing tips on the warning signals related to bulimia. Regardless, I feel it must be done as I believe it is important if a parent or relative suspects a person of having the disorder that they can qualify their suspicions with fact. Without substantial proof, denial will likely accompany the accusation and the concerned party will have forfeited any chance at breaking down the barrier.

Warning signals are listed in three different forms - emotional, physical, and material.

The emotional and physical signs are:

EMOTIONAL

- Depression
- Temperamental
- Voluntary isolation from others
- Distress
- Spiritless
- Indifference
- Excessive concern about weight
- Fear of gaining weight

PHYSICAL

- Slow or sustained muscular development
- Sluggishness
- Red gums
- Dizziness
- A complaint of sensitivity to cold and hot food
- Excessive concern towards health

- Increase complaints of pains in several regions of the body (primarily the lower back)
- Abdominal cramps
- Irregular menstrual cycles
- Unsteady weight
- Protrusion of muscles in the lower part of the back

OTHER SIGNS TO BE AWARE OF:

- Dry skin
- Abnormal variation of electrical current of the heartbeat
- Muscle spasms caused by mineral deficiency
- Depression
- Rapid and irregular heartbeat
- Body fat below normal (at times)
- Electrolyte imbalance
- Sensitivity to cold

It is however impossible to be sure that any of the above protests are linked directly to bulimia. The likely cause could be denied alternate excuses that could be used as a disguise. Due to this, I have included the following information composed of more concrete evidence. The individual desiring to acquire this substantiation must be prepared to delegate extra time to the investigation, and therefore these are primarily geared towards the people closest to the bulimic. They are as follows:

- Inconspicuous eating
- Hiding food
- Restrictive diets
- The rapid disappearance of food
- Frequently found food packages in garbage

- Frequent trips to the washroom (for bulimics who vomit, this usually occurs within 20 minutes after the meal to a maximum of one hour)
- A long period in the washroom
- Frequent toilet flushing at one visit
- Signs of spots around and on the inner rim of the toilet bowl (primarily on the water tank behind the seat)
- A long time with the tap water running (to muffle the sound)

I realize that some of the ominous signs are not pleasant, however, they are realistic and help in the discovery. I know. My mother became aware of my condition through many of these signs. The overwhelming evidence she placed before me made it difficult to deny the issue and create feasible excuses to counterbalance the proof.

If any of a combination of the above signals are apparent, the next step is the approach. How to do this as discussed in the next chapter.

THE APPROACH

So, the facts have been gathered and now the task of facing the person you believe to be bulimic is at hand. The whole ordeal has probably created a stream of feelings to flow within you. Anything from anger, to concern, to confusion, to fear but wait. Before you decide to take on the brave approach, you better regain access to a level mind. No progress will come out of a confrontation exploding with uncontrolled accusations. Sit down, relax, review your position, and set it in your mind to deal with this issue with patience and tact. And love.

The most important thing to bear in mind is that your discovery, backed by the evidence, is going to create another surge of emotions on the side. This means that someone is going to have to be able to remain calm, and it should not be expected to be the one you surprise with the evidence.

Often bulimics have said that parents are set in their ways and that they could not be changed or convinced into using methods other than the popular harsh negative retorts. I don't believe this. At least not if the concerned person is aware that this attitude could lead the bulimic into greater depression which may increase the purging. And the hiding. So, in sticking to my belief, regardless of popular adverse opinion, I am including this chapter to help educate parents and friends and teach them to deal with the person without hostility, but rather with compassion and effort to understand.

To be able to best understand bulimia, I advise parents and friends to research the topic to acquire proper knowledge of the psychological problems involved in this disorder. It is also advised to discuss the issue with a professional and enhance your comprehension of the suffering involved.

Be conscious that exposing awareness of the problem means primarily, in the eyes of the bulimic, that she is being robbed of the secrecy of her hidden behavior. The natural reaction to the confrontation is one of hate and betrayal and the surfacing of frenzy denials and perhaps even angered discourse. The other reaction may be one of aloofness and silence, as nothing said means nothing admitted.

A feasible approach is one in which the actual condition is not mentioned. Coming forth by way of expressing your belief that the person is going through some problems and advising them that you are there to help them may be the best choice. By avoiding direct accusations that someone has an eating disorder you are putting yourself in a better position to help. The last thing bulimics want here is someone telling them they have a problem. They often know this already. As well, by the time you figure it out, they're probably already entangled in the psychological problems that require delicate handling.

The proper steps are to present a willingness to maintain an open mind through a show of compassion, an effort of understanding and to discuss your desire to help and support the bulimic. Kindness is the most direct way to help. By showing acceptance of the person regardless of the disorder and by helping her to realize that you are willing to offer comfort and encouragement to create a more positive attitude, you're more likely to have her respond.

If the bulimic chooses not to open up and avoid any further discussion, the only way you can help is by continuing to monitor behavior without her knowing and by inducing a positive aura in her presence. To get annoyed is only causing you additional pain.

A few years ago, I discovered that someone close to me was purging her food. After a discussion with the other members of the family, the evidence became overwhelming. Now in a position of discoverer rather than discovered, I felt helpless. I wanted to face her and grab her and tell her the hell she was setting herself up for. But I knew better. After all, this confrontation wouldn't have worked for me, so why should I believe that it would work for her? I sat down and collected my thoughts. What should I do?

I took a chance. I approached her mother with the evidence and prayed that she would bring it up with her daughter. I coached her on the approach to take. One week later her mother advised me that the confrontation had proceeded as planned. The outcome had been a calm discussion and a calm denial. The subject was then dropped. Knowing this was not going to stop the disorder, I decided on my own accord to send anonymous information on the subject. I knew a second confrontation would jeopardize my desire to see her recover.

In the interim, a couple of visits to her home revealed further evidence that the purging hadn't ceased. Each time, anguish rose side of me. But again, I knew that lashing out was not the solution. Instead, I would discuss my own experience with bulimia in her presence, hoping it would create a positive influence.

Six months later, the signs of bulimia have ceased to show, but I could not be sure that the purging has. I could only hope.

I can now understand the despair and frustration of being 90% sure of someone being bulimic yet knowing that without the other 10% you have no case. The 10% being admission from the bulimic herself. I did not give up though until I was comfortable in knowing that the disorder had truly been conquered.

One reformed bulimic assured me that monitoring the behavior of the person as I had done was wrong. I disagreed. To discontinue keeping watch means you forfeit the ability to keep track of whether the danger still exists or not. It is easy for a bulimic to denounce this way of showing concern as warranted, for, after all, bulimia forever remains a personal secret, even though someone has voiced a suspicion. But I stressed that the watchful eye continues under caution, maintaining that it remains inconspicuous. If it is detected, it can produce, oddly enough, a lack of trust, the feeling that privacy is being invaded, and again, this may feed into the disorder. But by and large, do not stop caring enough to let the issue go.

Always be supportive of achievements the suspected person undergoes and work on building the esteem by focusing on the positive aspects of her personality and potential. Emphasize the fact that her life is controlled by her alone, not anyone else. If you become overprotective, however, this can stunt growth and induce feelings of helplessness which can cause loss of the self. Help to encourage the person to get involved in things she enjoys, be it painting, writing, or sports. But remember, you are to encourage her to do these, not tell her. You are in a position to encourage and support, not demand. In these endeavors, make sure to remain consistently sincere, as signs of pretentiousness can only obstruct your efforts.

On the subject of food, under no circumstance should you present food to a bulimic outside mealtime. Never nag them or force them to eat everything on their plate. Any such pressures just add to the condition. Meals should consist of proper quantities and 2nd helpings should not be offered. There are times that a bulimic will agree to have a second helping simply because they feel that this is the polite thing to do and if they do complete the second helping you can be assured that they will be visiting the washroom after the meal.

Overall, what must be understood is that the best result is when the decision to get help comes from the bulimic, not you. As such, if she opens up to you, your job is to encourage her to get this help and view it as a positive move, not when that should be regarded as shameful.

Just a note - once the issue has been surfaced, even the simple admission of suspicion can create paranoia in the bulimic. She becomes very aware of a watchful eye. Under these circumstances, she may either decrease the frequency of bingeing in your presence or using a more careful approach to her bulimia. The unfortunate thing is that it then becomes difficult to substantiate how severe the bulimia is. Even if it is the case that the purging has subsided, odds are this decrease is only temporary. It is induced by fear of being rediscovered, not from the desire to get well. When the bulimic feels the threat has passed, the disorder can recur, and at times it reestablishes itself at a more severe level. So, beware of this and do not let the issue pass at the first sign of possible recovery. The process involved in getting better rarely occurs overnight. Continue with your efforts to support the bulimic in the best way you know how until sufficient time has evolved to assure you that the behavior is under control. A possible sign of this is when the bulimic can openly discuss the problem with others. I know for me, once I had control of the situation, the topic did not inhibit me anymore. Once I reached full recovery, I was not ashamed to share the experience with others because it was an accomplishment that I was very proud of.

Another thing I caution is that if there is more than one child in the family, that care is taken in assuming that the disorder does not spread. I have known of a case where other family members, learning of the disorder of one, have voluntarily attempted to acquire the same capability. One of my sisters was one of these people. Luckily, she became aware of the dangers before it grew into a habit. This chain reaction may and often occurs amongst friends as well. It is probably the biggest reason why bulimia has since become widespread. So be aware of this and try to take the necessary steps to educate others on the negative aspects of the disorder before it is too late.

In summary, always remember to be patient, understanding, and encouraging. Don't allow yourself to be fooled by false signs of recovery and keep hoping that you can break the wall and clear the passage for communication. These are important. It is never easy to watch helplessly when someone we love torments themselves through self-destructive habits, but it is worse to contribute to the anguish already present. Your strength and building tolerance and understanding will be your most valuable asset.

In conclusion, there is an exception to my advice that I feel compelled to write about. This is in the case where the bulimic is in immediate physical danger. In such a case, do not hesitate to take it into your own hands and bring the person to the hospital right away for a complete examination. Hopefully, this will never come to pass.

"Reach high, for stars lie hidden in your soul. Dream deep, for every dream precedes the goal."

Pamela Vaull Starr

REACH FOR THE STARS

Before I end this book, I would like to discuss goals and achievements. It is said that we all need to achieve something to show others that we are able beings. It is something inherent in us. But it doesn't need to be grandiose. This could be to simply grow a beautiful flower, to paint, to write poems, or a book. But having a goal is important. It gives us something to look forward to, to reach for. Something to make tomorrow more worthwhile.

During my bulimia, I had lost sight of any goals and dreams I had held dear to me as an adolescent. This, I believe, greatly added to my final breakdown. For some reason, I had given up on dreaming and lost sight of any possibility of a future. Everything beyond the present was blocked. As I got better, I had to learn how to dream again. I had to learn how to set goals to work to make my tomorrow of greater value. As I learned to do this, I understood that the reestablishment of such treasured human qualities was possible. I could learn to dream again, to build goals to reach for, to work for today for a more promising tomorrow. But in the process, I also learned that these achievements and goals had to be within my grasp. I stopped setting impossible standards for myself and created new attainable standards.

Once I took the time to look inside myself, I saw wonderful desires, and soon I knew what it was I wanted to strive for. I wanted to be a writer. So, I dreamed I was. Next thing I knew I was taking courses in writing and sending out material. With this came, of course, the dreaded rejections. But to me, I made the collections of these as a hobby. I placed them in a binder where now and again I can flip through the pages and believe that they were a worthy step towards my eventual reaching my goal. I set no time limit. When it would happen, it would happen. The thing is I believed in it. That's all I needed to do - believe in my dream.

I now have three published books, (on with my character Hampy as per the illustration here), received a publisher's author award, contributed to a #1 Amazon Best Selling book, and followed my dream to become a Bulimia Recovery Coach and Masters Certified Handwriting Analyst and Graphotherapist. I have never stopped learning, doing, dreaming. I moved forward easier when I gave up my bulimia, even if back when I was bulimic, I learned how to be a functional one. I did manage through my 30 years of being one. But the last 10 years have been so much more fulfilling. I learned to deal with  my emotions healthily, and I have maintained my weight without dieting. I just listen to my mind and body now.

A big truth is, I got tired of having white spots in my eyes after a purge, of the exhaustion, of looking at that toilet and the many I saw in my life, of the rapid heartbeats that kept me wondering as I got older if they would cause a heart attack, of the sweats, of the cost, of the fear, but most of all, of the time it robbed from me because I chose to let it rob me.

I strongly advise that you do as I have. Look at your life closely and find a goal to pursue. The goal may be one that presents a risk of rejection, but without the risk, you gain nothing. All the while keep believing. And know that FULL recovery IS possible. If the "difficult change" is seen as positive, it won't be as difficult. Never let a step backward stop you from continuing. It may happen, so allow for it. But never stop dreaming. When you believe in your dream, it will, I assure you, come true.

Find that goal, the goal that defines satisfaction for you and your dream. Dream a lot. Don't let anyone tell you that dreamers are fools. It is those who cannot dream that are the fools. They are missing out on one of the greatest qualities we have been blessed with - not to mention one of the healthiest. Live for today but dream for tomorrow. Always strive for better, believe it can be and it will. I know this to be true because I am a believer.

In my entirety, I am a dreamer, believer, lover, and live'er. All because I have learned to let go of my "addiction", "crutch", "disorder" or whatever you want to call it, and risk. Try it, you'll be surprised how wonderful it is to be living again.

BONUS

I have added a portion of one of the Chapters of my book *(co-authored by Robert Max Wall)*, **Make Up Not Required – How To Brand The True YOU** which seems appropriate exercises for you. I hope you enjoy them. There is also a "free mini handwriting analysis" included in this.

CHAPTER 2

The Science of YOU

by LAURIEANN

What I mean by the "Science of YOU" *(Your Energy Is a Science and It Is Contagious)*

People don't see themselves as a "science" per se, but they are. Each individual is filled with energy and a force that makes up their being. That "being" is an element of science, and the main thing here is for you to define your scientific makeup. This is where you gain knowledge of your "self," and get to "know" yourself by splitting out the elements that make you who you are. This is the science of YOU.

What the heck am I talking about? Let me give you an example.

Who are you when you are alone? What are the things you like to do when there is no one around? How do you perceive yourself when you look in the mirror? Where do you go to find peace? When do you feel at your best? Why do you react a certain way to situations?

These are just some of the questions you can ask to define who you are.

Create your own questions. Start with the beginning word and finish the question. Then answer it.

Who____?

What____?

How____?

Where____ ?

When____?

Why____?

From the questions you asked, and how you answered them, write a paragraph on what you deduced from this exercise. This is the beginning of understanding more about your makeup—your science.

NOTES:

The Basics of the Science of YOU

You, the sum of the parts: parts of your being—your experiences, your actions, and reactions; your emotions, thoughts, physical desires, passions, and dislikes—a map of molecules, sometimes so wrapped up in a web, it creates confusion and overwhelm.

Make a list of positives now:

Who am I?

Who do I like?

What makes me smile?

What makes me laugh?

What fills me up?

What inspires me?

Build yourself around what inspires you about yourself, not what you think others are looking for.

The fact that you are *science* means that you are functioning with all the energy around you. To ensure success, you need to make sure you are focusing on the list above. The positive energy must outdo the negative by a long shot. It takes one small negative to distract you away from the positive. When that negative comes into your life, what you must do is turn your attention toward the list above. Focus on one of the elements. Meditate on it. This will reduce the confusion and overwhelm.

Characteristics That Define You *(To You)*

What are your main characteristics? The previous chapter listed the things that you enjoy. Now we will move on to your characteristics, your traits. We will do this in a different way than you would be used to.

It is an interesting fact that your handwriting is directly connected to the neurons in your brain; hence, your handwriting also will reflect characteristics that even you may not be aware of.

I am offering, in this chapter, a unique opportunity to further learn about these. Submit your handwriting to howtohaveyourcake.com@gmail.com, and I will then send you back a brief list of your main characteristics.

To do so, write with a blue ballpoint pen, on a blank piece of paper, the following:

The crazy purple monkey did not want to go to the zoo. "Why should I go to the zoo?" he asked.

"Because you need to go home," you said to him.

With this, finish off with your signature, and send it along. Remember, the paper has to be blank, and you must use a blue ballpoint pen. Any submission that does not follow these instructions will not receive a response. I say this because accuracy is important, and to be more accurate, these rules must be in place.

Just to let you know, I am a certified handwriting analyst and have done over 500 handwriting analysis reports. I will also enjoy getting your feedback, which you can do on my website as well after you receive your short report.

Also, on the website, will be the option to get further information about your characteristics, and if desired, a longer report, which can help you to further succeed at your business.

Here are a few further notes in defining yourself to look at:

Acts of kindness

____

Being born a

____

Going without, yet

____

Past challenges conquered

____

Parents' influence made me

____

And create your own:

____

____

____

I look forward to engaging with you.

Moments That Defined You

What were your fondest memories as a child? Was there anything specific that happened to you in your teen years, or recently, that changed your life, changed your mindset, or changed a part of you? Is there something you hold strong to and will not sway?

I know, as a child, I was very exuberant, and I loved to show off, until the age of 3 and a half. At that point, my mother had my sister, and my spotlight as the youngest and the baby of the family was removed. That point in my life changed my character. I became much more of a recluse and enjoyed my own company much more. I did have friends and enjoyed them, but I also liked being alone. This went on for most of my life. I was shy, but once you got to know me, you couldn't shut me up.

As a teen, I was very much into sports and cheerleading. This brought me out of my shell somewhat, regarding the fear of what others thought, but that fear was still there. It consumed me most of my life.

Does anyone relate to these? Are you a middle child? Were you bullied? Were you spoiled and never fearful? Were you fearful but did it anyway?

Interestingly, we all have moments that define us, and those moments are treasures when *branding the true you* because you are going to be sharing stories about those moments. So, list 10 here to start. We will take this further in a future chapter.

1

2

3

4

5

6

7

8

9

10

What Do You Love Most About "You?"

Noting what you love most about yourself is quite often hard to do. To brand YOU, it is of the utmost importance to find at least a couple of things that you love most about yourself. You will not shine if you don't have that ability to say what it is that you are great at—what makes you look in that mirror in the morning and say, "Let's do this." It takes knowing those parts of you that you love most to get you through tough times too!

Let me give you an example. I have struggled with believing in myself for years. I always thought I was not good enough, or pretty enough, or smart enough. My self-esteem was low for so long. Even married and with children, I still struggled.

Don't get me wrong. I was happy, and I did very well academically because I forced myself to, and I had ambition and always took the road less travelled. I was a literary agent at the age of 24, and even the vice president of the Toronto branch of the Canadian Author's Association, as well as the editor of their newsletter, which I printed on my old computer, a Tandy EX that had no hard drive. I was driven. I joined volunteer groups.

As life progressed, I lost my business by following my husband at the time; but I learned a lot by being his office manager, teaching him about accounting, which made him CFO, and I also did his marketing for 10 years. Then they fired me—conflict of interest.

I turned it around and became the executive director of a not-for-profit that helped people start their own businesses. And here is the story. I went into that interview not really feeling that I deserved to be in that capacity. But what helped was that I was very involved with the Chamber of Commerce, and I was on the board of directors. That got me the career opportunity.

And as great as that felt, and I felt my self-esteem was rising, I was in a relationship that didn't help. It was one where the love of my life wanted me to do well, but then felt I was not doing enough as a mother and a wife.

That relationship ended with great pain, at the same time that I lost my job due to lack of funding.

So, I was divorced and bought an auto repair company 4 years later, having been now engaged in the automotive industry. Three years later, the recession happened.   But it wasn't all about the recession. It was partially my fault too. In trying to beat the recession, I over-invested in possibilities instead of trying to fix what was bleeding. Not failure but another lesson; but again, I lost the love for myself.

Here is where I found it: when I changed my mindset—when I looked at my achievements rather than the things I didn't manage to make the way I wanted them to be.

Marriages dissolve, businesses dissolve, but the fact that you take a chance on love or business doesn't dissolve. It builds character.

So here, write down the achievements you have in your life (e.g., family, business, volunteering). In the end, I can ensure that you will see that what left your hands never left your heart, or your head, with what you learned from it all.

These are my top 5, but you will write your top 10!! And submit them to our website!

- Author of *Hampy* (created when I was 18; published when I was 48; www.hampy.ca)
- Youngest VP of the Toronto Canadian Authors Association
- The first one in my circle of friends to have a sole proprietorship (literary agency) at 24
- Self-employed on the side for 33 years; Pinnacle Award for most volunteering; president of the Chamber of Commerce (not an easy task at 38)
- Adamant about marrying my first true love; together for 22 years, with three children; divorced with no regrets

Your turn:

1. ____

2. ____

3. ____

4. ____

5. ____

6. ____

7. ____

8. ____

9. ____

10. ____

OTHER READINGS

Below I have listed other books you may want to go over. I have found books about the disorder not always the most valuable, I've also listed some books which have no reference to bulimia but are inspirational and can help emotionally by inducing a better understanding of what life is about.

Enjoy!

Suggested readings and references in this book:

Minding The Body, Mending The Mind, Dr. Joan Borysenko Ph.D., Addison-Wesley Publishers Ltd., Don Mills, Ontario

Living, Loving & Learning, Dr. Leo Buscaglia, Ballantine Books, New York *(permission received to use the quotes from Dr. Leo Buscaglia's book)*

The Magic Question, Bart Baggett, Empresse Publishing, California

Taming Your Gremlin, Rick Carson, Harper Collins Publishers, New York

Understanding Your Immune System, Morra E. Potts, Avon Books, New York

The Food Book, B. Stern, et al, Bookmark Books, New York

Fat Is A Feminist Issue, Susan Orbach, Paddington Press Ltd., New York

Other books by the author available on Amazon:

Hampy, The Book
www.hampy.ca
Released 2010©
An illustrated book on bullying, and finding yourself.

Make Up Not Required – How To Brand The True YOU
www.makeupnotrequired.com
Released September 2020©
Special techniques on how to realize the "true YOU" to gain trust and loyalty in your Brand.

1 Habit For Successful Entrepreneurs – Contributing Author
Released November 2020©
150 Entrepreneurs share their 1 Habit for success and their one "unhabit".
Featured authors Forbes Riley and Steve Samblis

Soon To Be Released: Sherri's World – The story of a bulimic spanning 30 years. *(Fiction, Based On A True Story)*   More information will be posted on www.bullimiaddict.com.

www.ingramcontent.com/pod-product-compliance
Lightning Source LLC
Chambersburg PA
CBHW060933050726
47592CB00003B/941